ACPL ITEM
DISCARDED

3 1833 01645 9387

641
Day, Glenn, 1946-
Crab cookery coast to coast

P9-EDO-500

DO NOT REMOVE
CARDS FROM POCKET

7/23/92

ALLEN COUNTY PUBLIC LIBRARY

FORT WAYNE, INDIANA 46802

You may return this book to any agency, branch,
or bookmobile of the Allen County Public Library.

DEMCO

Crab Cookery Coast To Coast

Jimmys,
Jonahs,
Busters & Blues

Glenn Day

 The Crossing Press • Freedom, CA 95019

Allen County Public Library
Ft. Wayne, Indiana

My special thanks to the many people who shared their invaluable recipes, experience, advice, and inspiration, including my parents; my sisters, Angie, Margaret, and Jeanie; my nieces, Melissa Englert, Sarah Samson, and Catherine Samson; and my Aunt Ann Andrew; also, Ann Harding Bonneau, Shari and Jim Clark, Chef John Gilbertson, Linda Haskins, Annette Reddell Hegen, Dalton Hobbs, Arlene and Paul Hodge, Alicia and Wayne Locke, C.P. McIlhenny, Polly Moore, Mrs. Brooks Peterson, Buck Pierson, Don Ray, Governor Ann Richards, Deanna Ryan, Betty Shaw, Kathy Shaw, Kara Shelton, Tom Simon, Ann Thompson, Marilyn Pierson Van Zandt, Charles Watson, Andrea Wallace, and Ronald Winton.

I also wish to thank the Alaska Seafood Marketing Institute, Florida Bureau of Seafood Marketing, Louisiana Seafood Promotion and Marketing Board, Marine Advisory Service, Texas A&M University, Maryland Department of Economic and Community Development, Maryland Office of Seafood Marketing, National Marine Fisheries Service, New England Fisheries Development Association, Oregon State Seafood Marketing Program, and United States Department of Agriculture for their invaluable assistance in the preparation of this book.

Copyright © 1982 by Glenn Day
Cover art & design, and interior art by Anne Marie Arnold
Printed in the U.S.A.

Library of Congress Cataloging-in-Publication Data
Day, Glenn, 1946-
    Crab cookery coast to coast: Jimmys, Jonahs, Busters, and Blues / by Glenn Day.
        p. cm.
    Includes index.
    ISBN 0-89594-530-4 (cloth)   ISBN 0-89594-529-0 (pbk.)

    1. Cookery (Crabs) 2. Cookery, American. 3. Crabs—United States. I. Title.
TX754.C83D39 1992   91-45113
641.6'94—dc20   CIP

Contents

Preface

My fondest memory of dining on crab is not at an elegantly set table lit by moonlight, but sitting on a wharf with a few well chosen friends. It was at Port Aransas on the Texas Gulf coast, but the same evening could just have easily been spent on the Chesapeake Bay or in the Florida keys or on the shore of one of the shallow bays in northern California.

This recipe for a good meal and a great time begins with two crab traps, a large pot, and a Coleman stove. We set out in late afternoon, stopping at a market along the way to fill a basket with French bread, white wine, butter, and lemons. At the fish counter we picked up some scrap heads for bait. On the way out the door we added a newspaper chosen with greater regard for thickness than journalistic excellence.

We headed for an out-of-the-way pier. This one was seldom crowded, had a picnic table at the end, and, best of all, was a good spot for crabbing. In no time, we moved our equipment to the picnic table and set to work in earnest. The traps were laid out, baited, and dropped into the gulf. The newspaper was torn apart, spread over the table, and weighted at the edges to withstand the Gulf breezes. We lit the stove and set a large pot of salt water to boil. On the edge of a low burner we set the butter to melt.

Hardest of all, we waited to give the crabs time to find our traps. Waiting on crabs is thirsty business, so we passed the wine around. After about fifteen minutes we pulled the two traps up. Luck was with us. Each trap held a nice fat crab. Neither of the crabs was especially friendly, but we had not come to pay a social call. We upended the traps and dropped the crabs directly into the boiling pot, then returned the traps to the sea.

Another fifteen minutes passed, and it was time to to take out the boiled crabs and to recheck the traps. The crabs came from the pot bright red, ready to eat. We drew straws for the lucky two who got to eat first. While the two winners set to work with nut crackers and picks, the others turned their attention back to the traps. Two more frisky crabs had accepted the invitation to come ashore and they were appropriately welcomed. In the meantime, lemon juice had been added to the butter for dipping and the French bread was in pieces on the table.

As one of the people who had to eat on the second shift, I am pleased to say that the first shift was gracious enough to share while my crab was cooking. It is not a reflection on my friends' natural charity to say that the mournful expression on my face may have prompted their generosity.

At the end of a delightful evening, we wrapped everything up in the used newspapers and tossed the table leavings in a barrel at the end of the pier. It was the sort of kitchen cleanup that even I find agreeable.

Of course, every meal is not a finger-licking occasion nor is a newspaper always the best choice for a tablecloth. Don't we all sometimes want candlelight and soft music? I do. I've included recipes in this book fit for the the most elegant table, such as Crab Meat Stuffed Coho Salmon (from John Clancy's Restaurant in New York), Crabs Girardeau Flambé, and a very stylish Gazpacho with Crab Meat. I have also included a selection of the best crab cake recipes I have ever tasted. People who know how much I like crab cakes will immediately appreciate the care I took with this portion of the book, and I sincerely hope you relish this unique American favorite as much as I do.

On other occasions I have found that a tasty crab dish is just what I need for a buffet item, the sort of finger food that people can enjoy standing up without having to worry about butter spots on their ties or blouses. (Incidentally, if you have never had a butter spot on your tie or blouse, you are probably not enjoying your crab meat with sufficient vigor.) Still, there is a time and a place for everything, and you will find several spot-free recipes in this book, including one from Ann Richards, the governor of Texas and a veteran of countless buffet lines and handshake fests while on the campaign trail.

Any crab meat commonly available at your local market can be used for the recipes in this book. The color, taste, and texture of the dish may vary somewhat, however, depending on the variety of crab used and whether you use lump meat, claw meat, or some other form.

While testing these recipes, I used fresh herbs unless noted otherwise. You can easily convert these fresh herbs to dried by allowing 1/2 teaspoon dry herbs for each tablespoon of fresh herbs. This is the standard used in most cookbooks. However, I have found that dried herbs cannot approximate the flavor of fresh herbs; often when I use dried herbs, I use somewhat more than the amount for which the recipe calls.

I hope that you will take these recipes as just the beginning of your journey to a superb dish; however, please remember that crab meat is very delicately flavored. If you are just starting to experiment with seasonings, use a minimum and then add more as your palate dictates.

Introduction

History of Crabs in the United States

In the United States, crab is one of the most popular seafoods. This was not always so, for many of the first European settlers did not realize the bounty lying just below the surface in the shallow bays and estuaries. But crabs were an important food in the diets of coastal dwelling Native Americans long before the coming of the Europeans.

The English settlement led by Captain John Smith in 1608 lay immediately south of Chesapeake Bay. Although food was so scarce that starvation threatened, the stubborn colonists flatly refused to follow the lead of Native Americans and fish for the crabs that were literally crawling out of the water. Only Captain Smith's laying down of his famous rule "He who will not work shall not eat," prompted the settlers to begin crabbing.

The English who landed at Plymouth Rock were more accepting. Southeastern New England was ruled by various tribes of the Wampanoag Confederacy. One of these was the Pamet, a tribe especially adept at fishing the Atlantic coastal waters. They taught the Europeans how to build crab traps from vines and sticks. The crabs taken in these traps proved to be a rich and popular source of food for the colonists. One contemporary description of the first Thanksgiving feast mentions boiled crabs.

A similar story unfolded far to the south, where Florida's Seminole tribe shared with the strangers their way of cooking crabs. The Seminoles boiled crabs along with small oranges that grew in profusion throughout the region. Reports by the explorers recall that the crabs had superior flavor and that huge feasts of boiled crabs were common.

Early Texas explorers recorded that the Coahuiltecan and Karankawa tribes, though primitive by the standards of tribes inhabiting the coast of Mexico, were skilled in fishing crabs from sandy bottoms and mud flats. They favored catching crabs either in traps or by running seines along the bottom. These tribes taught the white men.

On the Pacific coast of the Northwest, English settlers entering the area of Puget Sound discovered that the Clallam, Hadia, and other tribes in the area were thoroughly familiar with the rich and delicate flavor of the Dungeness crab, which they caught in large quantities in traps almost identical to the ones we use today. The English colonists adopted the native methods and soon were adding crabs to their tables.

Along the coastal areas where crabs were most abundant, they became to be a regular portion of the colonial diet. Over time, classic, distinctively American recipes and traditions evolved, often tied to their place of origin. The boiled or steamed crab of the Chesapeake Bay became one of the major attractions of the region. In season, the Chesapeake's soft-shell crab, prepared over grills or in broilers, was hailed as the world's finest.

In sophisticated Charleston, she-crab soup was a delicacy par excellence and was served at the city's best tables in bowls of the finest English china. In some quarters, she-crab soup recipes took on somewhat the air of a state secret. Recipes were handed down from mother to daughter and from cook to cook with an air of mystery and many pledges of secrecy. Incredible as it may seem today, in the South of yesterday the wooing away of a valued cook or the "borrowing" of a treasured recipe could be such an affront to honor that it resulted in breached social relations.

People who breathed the more free and easy air of the old sin-city of New Orleans seldom took such umbrage when dishes turned up tasting suspiciously similar to their own treasured recipes. They prepared crabs in all the ways favored by the people of the day, and in addition cooked gumbo, one of Louisiana's unique contributions to American cuisine. Perhaps one reason that gumbo recipes were not more closely guarded is that few people who are genuine artists in its preparation make it precisely the same way twice. It is not unusual for outstanding gumbo cooks to declare, truthfully, that they have no recipe. Gumbo, like jazz, cries out for improvisation. And the chefs of New Orleans have improvised so well and for so long, that a steaming bowl of gumbo, rich with crab meat and shrimp, is world famous, an obligatory treat for travelers to the Crescent City.

Louisiana people, perhaps with reason, claim that the mud bottoms of the Louisiana delta give a distinctive taste to the crabs that live there. The delta is formed from soil washed from the very heartland of the United States into the Mississippi River. The silt is then carried the width of our nation to be deposited in Louisiana. If any soil in America is entitled to the benefit of the doubt for special taste, this is it. All I know for sure is that deciding this question for yourself will be an enjoyable experience.

Not surprisingly, the people of the Pacific coast developed their own special dishes and traditions around the rich taste of crab meat. Perhaps the most famous is the cioppino seafood stew that originated in the docks of San Francisco. Cioppino is probably the premier traditional dish using the Dungeness crab. A bowl of fresh, hot cioppino served with crunchy French bread and a glass of chilled wine is a treat fit for a king. And best of all, from a cook's perspective, cioppino is fun to prepare. Like gumbo, cioppino readily accepts a wide variety of fish and other ingredients and encourages the cook to give free reign to his or her imagination.

And while Americans were happily developing traditional dishes and exploring new ways to add crabs and crab meat to their tables, how were crabs harvested? Pretty much the same way they had been for 300 years, which is to say, slowly. With only minor improvements, crab fishing was conducted in a way that would have been familiar to the original inhabitants of Plymouth Colony. Small traps, nets, and lines brought home most of the catch. Crabbing was essentially an endeavor for amateur fishermen and for a few small commercial operators.

Slow, labor-intensive harvesting of crabs was possible because, as good as crabs were, the market for crabs was really quite small. Crabs spoiled so rapidly that they could be marketed only to the local population. As people moved inland, they left crabs and crab dishes behind as lost but well-remembered delicacies. But in the years following the Civil War, forces were in motion that would change all that. From a slow beginning, commercial marketing of crabs and crab meat began to change at an increasing rate.

Change was made possible by improvements in transportation and refrigeration, two early beneficiaries of the industrial revolution. Fortunes were at stake. A vast market for crabs and all sorts of shellfish existed beyond the sight and smell of the sea, a market heretofore untapped because the means did not exist to deliver fresh seafood over long distances. New inventions opened this market. And it was a market the United States was uniquely able to fill, because the United States enjoyed waters filled with a larger variety of crabs and other shellfish than any other country in the world.

The first of the shellfish family to take advantage of rapid transportation and improved refrigeration was the lobster. And when lobster came into its own, it was like an explosion. The riches created almost overnight by the new machine age brought into being a class of merchants and manufacturers for whom price was no object. These new world princes flocked to the most expensive dining rooms and resorts available, and changed their loyalties as new and more impressive facilities were built. Restaurateurs strived to provide the most lavish menus and exquisite new dishes.

The nation's most renowned restaurants schemed and offered bribes for outstanding chefs and their special lobster recipes in a rivalry the old Charleston matrons would have understood. There was more than a touch of East Coast/West Coast one-upmanship at work, and for a time the succulent lobsters of Maine were shipped in special holding tanks on the transcontinental railroad to San Francisco, where hotels and dining rooms second to none were constructed. New York was nearer the source of prime lobsters, and soon New York's great restaurants such as Delmonico's, the Knickerbocker Grill, Sherry's, and others claimed (wrongly) that New York was the only place in the nation where gentlemen and great ladies could enjoy a properly prepared lobster.

As the majestic lobster paved the way, the crab followed. Enterprising tradesmen soon realized that the same ice-filled railroad cars that carried lobsters to the tables of Manhattan, Chicago, St. Louis, Denver, Philadelphia, Cincinnati, and the great resorts of upstate New York could carry crabs as well. New items were added to menus, new recipes were developed. Crab dishes and crab sauces were added to the menus of the most prominent restaurants of the land. The crab had broken free of the seacoast, upholding the classic definition of a necessity, that is, a luxury once tasted.

Today the catching, processing, and shipping of crabs would be unrecognizable to a crabber of a hundred years ago. Canned and pasteurized crab meat has been added to grocery shelves. The crab trade has changed dramatically even in the last 10 years. In the larger cities, including cities far inland, it is no longer unusual to find crabs sold alive, although it is still true that the farther inland the harder one must look.

To supply the huge demand for crab meat, the crab industry has become more capital intensive, replacing wherever possible the tedious handwork that characterized the industry from its inception. The most revolutionary step in the harvesting of crabs is the development of the floating processing plant, a combination fishing ship and processing factory.

Processing ships make it possible to catch, process, and freeze the crab meat in one location in a brief time, often only minutes after the crab leaves the water. Crab meat processed on one of these floating factories can be frozen at its peak freshness and that freshness preserved until delivered to the consumer.

In seafood, consumer satisfaction relates almost directly to freshness, and so freshness in turn relates almost directly to the price a fisherman can obtain for his catch. Since modern processing techniques result in crab meat being delivered in better condition to the consumer, a better price can be realized by the fishermen. Waste from spoiled crab is also reduced. How many fishermen in the past encountered mechanical problems or the vagaries of weather on the way to a dockside processing plant and so stood by helplessly while their catch spoiled? This is the economic engine that drives the huge investment in floating processing plants, and makes possible the increasing quality of crab meat available in American markets. Even the older, dockside processing facilities have been upgraded and modernized to handle the demands of the market for freshness and quality.

But faster, high quality processing of crabs is only half the story. The other half is getting the crab meat to market, and that is the revolution of handling and transportation.

The role that interstate highways have played in placing virtually every village in the United States within convenient driving range of refrigerated trucks is an old story. The new story is the impact of wide-body jets and modern computer systems on the transportation of fresh, top quality crab meat and other seafood.

Airline freight rates dropped significantly in the wake of airline deregulation. About the same time, airlines began flying newly purchased wide-body jets, airplanes with cargo holds large enough to accommodate containerized shipment. Seafood merchants were among the first to seize the new opportunities these changes made possible. In the 1980s, it became economically feasible to ship seafood in quantity to distant markets by air, delivering crab meat to inland markets with a freshness never before possible.

The increased use of smaller and more versatile computers played a role in this marketing revolution. Computers made it possible to keep up with crab catches from the time they were pulled from the water until they were delivered to market. Computers monitored containerized shipments on air carriers that maintained rigid schedules of departures and arrivals. The risk that crabs would sit for hours awaiting shipment, or would be spoiled while waiting for transportation from the loading dock to the market, was reduced to acceptable levels.

So what does this revolution in crab marketing mean? It means that it is possible to ship live crabs many miles inland to areas that only a few years ago had never seen a live crab. Larger supermarkets (and oriental grocers) have been especially ready to offer this new service to their customers.

It means that some crabs, such as the king or the tanner, that previously were available only near the point of capture or in larger cities, are now generally available to American tables. You have probably seen these in your market. They are usually marketed as king crab legs.

Most of all, the revolution in crab marketing means that the quality and freshness of the crab meat available to you is rising and will continue to rise. It means that you have new choices. It means that it is easy to add crab to your diet almost anywhere in the United States without having to settle for an inferior product. For people who live inland, the taste of crab is no longer purely a vacation time treat or a food that must be enjoyed in restaurants. Crab meat has become a food you can bring to your own table, seasoned and prepared to your taste. Like so much of the bounty of the U.S., it is as near as your grocer.

Geographical Locations of Commercially Available Crabs

blue crab	=	Cape Cod to southern tip of Texas; very numerous in Chesapeake Bay region
Dungeness	=	southern tip of Alaska to southern tip of California; very numerous in Monterey Bay, California
golden crab	=	Gulf of Mexico off Texas
green crab	=	Maine to New Jersey
Jonah crab	=	Maine to Long Island
king crab	=	off coast of Alaska
land crab	=	Florida
oyster crab	=	Pacific Northwest
red crab	=	Atlantic off New York; Pacific off California
rock crab	=	Pacific off mid-California; Atlantic off Virginia coast
snow crab	=	off coast of Alaska
stone crab	=	Florida
tanner crab	=	off coast of Alaska

Seasons When Crabs Are Plentiful

Legal seasons vary and in some states do not exist at all. The following crabs are available in these seasons:

blue crab	=	late spring to early fall
Dungeness	=	winter
soft-shell	=	late spring to early fall
king crab	=	winter
stone crab	=	year-round since they live in such warm waters

Cleaning and Cooking
Crab Meat

The choicest and freshest crab meat will be obtained by picking the meat from a crab just plucked steaming hot from the cooker.

Cleaning a crab always looks hard to a novice. It is not. With only a little thought, anyone could do it with no instruction at all. Following directions, it is simple.

The only crabs you are likely to clean or pick are the crabs that come near shore, such as the blue crab and the Dungeness crab. If you catch or happen to find at market one of the lesser known crabs such as the Jonah (also known as the rock crab), calico, or red crab, simply clean it as you would a blue crab.

Soft-shell crabs are not picked but are eaten whole after cleaning. For instructions for cleaning soft-shell crabs, see page 25.

Picked crab meat in the market is increasingly machine processed, but a large part of the crab harvest is still done by hand. Most of the remaining hand processing plants are small, family-owned enterprises employing only a few people and processing the catch from a single port or area, sometimes from a single fisherman. The crab meat is sold to large wholesalers, to local merchants, or in nearby large cities to retail purchasers whom the processor knows.

I toured one of these small, hand-processing plants. I wanted to see it while I still could, for the economics of the crab industry no longer favor small processors. Crabs here were cooked in the same way as you would at home but on a larger scale, in big open kettles. After cooking, the crabs were placed onto a conveyer belt moving down the center of a long narrow table. The workers, specialists with amazing skill, were seated on each side of the table. Each crab picker had a small work area about the size of a large chopping board.

As crabs moved down the conveyer pickers would grab a crab and move it to their work area for cleaning. These people could clean the crab and extract the crab meat faster than my tired old eyes could follow. Claws disappeared down one of a series of holes in the chopping board. Lump meat went down another hole, and other portions of meat down still another. Throughout the process, waste products were discarded into a stainless steel barrel. In moments, the crab was gone, reduced to waste and to picked meat, and another crab had taken its place.

Blue Crabs and Other Hard-Shell Crabs

The blue crab is the most common crab found in U.S. Atlantic and Gulf waters. The Chesapeake is especially noted for the size and quality of blue crab. Blues have tender, sweet meat and are often sold alive in markets. They are about 4 to 6 inches when fully grown and weigh about 5 ounces. Unlike their larger West Coast cousin, the Dungeness crab, blues must be steamed or boiled before cleaning. When raw, the blue crab is almost impossible to clean.

Cooking Blue Crabs

For boiled crabs, wash the crabs under fresh running water. Be sure that they are all alive and active. Bring water to a rapid boil in a pot. Drop the crabs into the water. Cover the pot and reduce the heat. Simmer for 15 minutes, or until the crabs turn bright red. Remove the crabs from the boiling water and serve immediately, or pour cold water over the crabs and clean them.

For steamed crabs, put a rack in the bottom of a large pot. The rack must be placed so that the crabs will not touch the boiling liquid. Cover the bottom of the pot with 1 inch of water. When the water is boiling vigorously, arrange the crabs on the rack. Reduce heat and steam until the crabs turn bright red, about 15 minutes. Remove from the pot. If not served hot, the crabs should be rinsed in cold water and cleaned.

Cleaning a Blue Crab

A crab can look formidable. How, you think, can I possibly even get into that, let alone clean it? Fortunately, it is not hard. There are only a few things you need to know, and these are quickly learned.

1. Break the large pincer claws and the legs from the body. Crack the claws with a nutcracker or mallet and remove the meat. The blue crab's legs will not contain enough meat to bother with.

Cleaning a Cooked Blue Crab

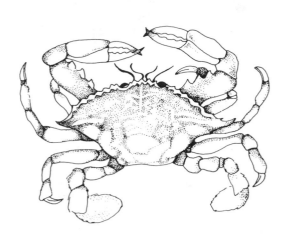

The choicest and freshest crab meat will be obtained by picking the meat from a crab just plucked steaming hot from the cooker.

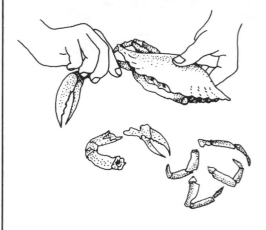

1. Break the large pincer claws and the legs from the body. Only the claws will contain enough meat to bother removing with a nutcracker or mallot.

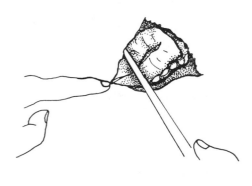

2. Turn the crab upside down. Locate the tail apron that folds under the body from the back. Break it away and pull it straight back from the body of the crab. The intestinal vein of the crab should pull away with it.

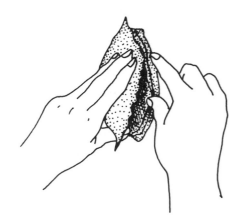

3. Loosen the top shell by prying under the shell midway along the back edge with fingers, a short knife, or a screwdriver. The shell should come off with a steady, firm pull.

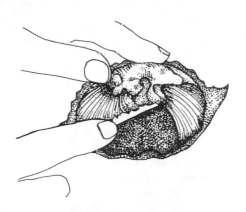

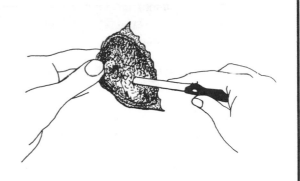

4. Wash away or remove the gills, intestines and spongy matter from the top side of the crab. Cut away the top of the crab's inner skeleton. This will expose the inner body meat.

5. Pick out all the exposed meat with a nut pick, the point of a knife, or some other pointed tool. Be sure to cut out the large lump of white meat in the back of the crab from each side.

Blue Crab

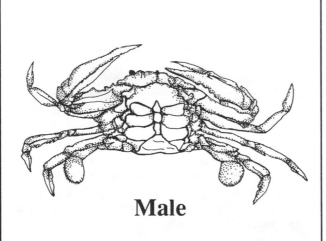

Male

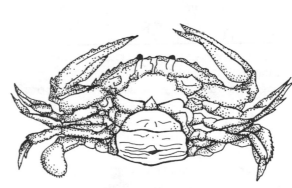

Female

2. Turn the crab upside down. Locate the tail flap (apron) that folds under the body from the back. Break it away and pull it straight back from the body of the crab. The intestinal vein of the crab should pull away with it.

3. Loosen the top shell of the crab by prying under the shell midway along the back edge. Fingers, a short knife, or a screwdriver can be used to gently work the body loose from the shell. Pull to remove. The shell should come off with a steady, firm pull. Save the top shell for stuffing, if you like.

4. Wash away or remove the gills, intestines, and spongy matter from the top side of the crab.

5. Cut away the top of the crab's inner skeleton. This will expose the inner body meat.

6. Pick out all the exposed meat with a nut pick, the point of a knife, or some other pointed tool.

7. Be sure to cut out the large lump of white meat in the back of the crab on each side. This is the muscle that operates the blue crab's swimming fin. It is the most choice part of the blue crab. If you are cleaning a Jonah or one of the other small walking crabs, this pocket of meat will not be present.

Dungeness Crabs

Dungeness crab is the largest and most popular crab fished from Pacific coastal waters. Its meat is tender and richly flavored. A mature Dungeness crab may have a shell up to 12 inches or larger and crabs of 2 to 3 pounds are not unusual.

Dungeness crabs can be cleaned either before or after cooking. I like to clean the Dungeness after cooking, but this is a matter of preference. People who prefer to clean the Dungeness crab before cooking often maintain that the Dungeness is more flavorful than meat obtained by cleaning afterward. Some of the people who clean Dungeness after cooking simply do not choose to kill the crab directly but would rather plunge it into boiling water and deal with cleaning it after the crab is cooked.

I suggest that you decide for yourself the method that best suits you. I have tried Dungeness both ways and find both methods quite satisfactory. Rest assured, whether you clean the Dungeness crab before or after cooking it, you are sure to find people who will tell you that the other way is better.

Cleaning a Dungeness Crab before Cooking

1. Kill the crab by either piercing the crab between the eyes with a sharp knife or placing the crab on its back, placing a sharp knife along the middle of its underside, and striking the knife briskly with a hammer or mallet. This should be done immediately prior to cooking. Once the crab has been killed, it must be cleaned at once.

2. Turn the crab upside down. Locate the tail flap (apron) that folds under body from the back. Break it away and pull it straight back from the body of the crab. The intestinal vein of the crab should pull away with it.

3. Separate the front from the back of the crab by pulling the crab apart or by pushing the top shell of the crab against a table top or the edge of a cutting board and pushing sharply. The top shell should pop off the crab and expose the inside. This seems harder to do than it actually is. After cleaning only a few crabs, removing the top shell will become second nature.

4. Break the right and left halves of the crab into two pieces.

5. Rinse the crab halves under running water to remove the internal organs. Remove and discard the gills and any mouth parts.

To cook the cleaned crab, rinse the crab, including the body cavity, under running water. Reduce the heat to allow the water to simmer. Place the crabs in the water, cover, and simmer until the crabs turn bright red, about 15 minutes. Since the body cavity of a cleaned crab is open to boiling water, a cleaned Dungeness does not require a rolling boil for cooking. When the crabs are cooked, remove them from the pot, drain, and pat dry. Serve the crabs immediately or rinse them in cold water and pick out the meat for later.

Boiling Dungeness Crabs before Cleaning

To boil Dungeness crabs before cleaning, you have merely to keep the crabs alive and active until they go into

Stone Crab

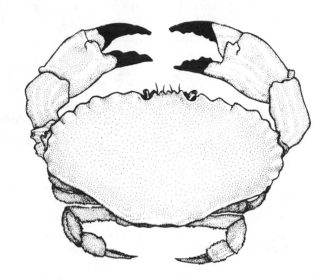

Dungeness Crab

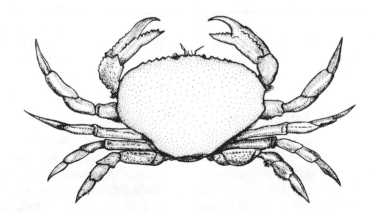

the pot. Rinse the crabs in running water, then drop each crab into the pot head first. Cover and continue boiling until the crabs turn bright red, 10 to 13 minutes.

Remove the crabs from the boiling water. Serve immediately or wash with cold water before cleaning. When you pick out the crab meat, remove the cartilage, membranes, and bits of shell before serving. The meat should come out cleanly, but nut picks or some other pointed tool may be useful.

Stone Crabs

Since it is illegal to take whole stone crabs from the water, it is unlikely that you will need to cook or clean the whole crab. You would not find it a worthwhile activity anyway, because the stone crab lives up to its name in hardness. Cracking the body of a stone crab is extremely difficult. In any case, the meat inside the body of the stone crab is hardly worth the effort.

The meat of the stone crab is contained in its claws. To clean and pick the meat from the claws of the stone crab, first cook the claw meat by steaming, or plunge into boiling water and boil for 15 minutes or until the crabs turn bright orange red. Either eat the meat in the claws hot or rinse the claws with cold water before cracking and picking out the meat.

Almost all stone crabs sold at market have been caught by commercial fishermen in boats equipped to cook the claws immediately and store the catch on ice. This attention to quality and freshness had paid rich dividends, not only for the fishermen, but also for consumers inland who now find stone crab claws in markets that only a few years before had never seen them.

Buying Crabs and Crab Meat

Live Crabs

If you are one of the lucky ones who lives where you can purchase live crabs, take advantage of your opportunity. Crab meat is like most foods—the fresher the better—and you can't get any fresher than the live crab. Of the four most commercially important crabs, blue, Dungeness, king, and stone crabs, only blue and Dungeness are offered alive.

When buying live crabs, you should always purchase them as near as possible to the time you will be cooking them. The crabs should be alive and lively when you purchase them. Live crabs will keep for a day or perhaps two in the refrigerator, but after 6 to 8 hours mortality rates rise. If a crabs dies between the time you purchase it and the time you cook it, you have lost your meal.

Do not under any circumstances buy or cook a dead crab unless it was killed in the process of cleaning. When a crab dies, the enzymes in the digestive tract will begin to digest the crab itself. Once this process starts, harmful bacteria will quickly form. For the same reason, do not allow cooked crabs to come into contact with dead crabs, since the bacteria will migrate from the dead to the cooked ones.

Some people, perhaps those with dead crabs to sell, maintain that as long as the crab smells fresh and presents a good appearance that it is all right to cook it after it dies. I do not recommend it, and I do not know any first-rate cook who does.

Finding a dead crab when you are ready for a crab feast is a tragedy that would challenge the pen of Shakespeare. Far better to purchase your crab immediately before cooking, and avoid disappointment.

Look for crabs that are heavy in proportion to their size. When you shake the crab, it should not make a liquid sound. Common sense will tell you the reason for this. The crab grows until it bursts out of its skeleton, then it grows a new skeleton or shell with room for new growth. A crab near the end of its molting cycle will be more filled with meat than if it has just shed its shell and acquired a new, roomy one. If you buy a "light" crab by weight you will be paying for more water than meat, and if you buy by size you will get less meat for your money. Either way, buy a "heavy" crab.

There are two schools of thought as to the size crab you should buy. One school holds that the small ones are best because they taste better than the larger ones and because their meat is more tender. The other school holds that it does not take any longer to clean a large crab than a small one and that you get much more meat for your time.

Frankly, I am of two minds on the subject. When faced with the choice, I almost always favor buying the most fresh and lively crabs without respect to size. If pressed by equally lively crabs of unequal size, I usually buy the larger ones. I have not found the differences in taste and tenderness pronounced, and I like the larger pieces of meat the bigger crabs yield.

Many people consider the ideal size for a Dungeness crab to be 2 1/2 to 3 pounds, and a blue crab to be about 3/4 to 1 pound. The Dungeness crab, on average, should have about 33 percent of its weight in meat; a blue crab should yield about 15 percent. Blues should be most numerous and cheapest between June and October, while the Dungeness should be cheaper during the winter months.

If you have a choice, select female crabs over males. The flavor of the females is a bit sweeter. You can readily tell a female crab by the broad apron, or tail, tucked underneath the back of the crab.

Crabs are graded by size measured across the widest part of its body. Unfortunately, different dealers use various names for the same size crab. It is all very confusing and the only real defense is to remain alert and select crabs based on what you see, not on what you read. In defense of the fishmongers, the market for live crabs at the retail level is simply undeveloped. As the industry grows stronger and standards are made more uniform, most of the confusion will vanish.

If possible, avoid buying crabs after a storm or unusual turbulence in the water. Crabs are likely to be gritty after a disturbance of their habitat. This is why the most choice crabs are taken from the shallow, sluggish waters of protected bays and estuaries where the tides are slow and storm ravages are minimal.

Once you have selected your crabs, carry them home packed somewhat tightly. Crabs packed loosely will tend to fight and injure or kill one another. If you are carrying them in a paper bag, simply roll the bag snugly. Remember that the crabs have to breathe, and if you roll them in a plastic bag they will suffocate.

For best results once you get home, leave your crabs in the paper sack. Place a moist towel over the crabs. Set the sack inside a leakproof tray and set on a low shelf in the refrigerator. You need take no special care to stop the crabs from crawling all over your refrigerator; in the cold, still air, the crabs will almost invariably become inactive.

Crab Meat

Freshly Cooked Crab Meat

Freshly cooked crab meat, long available in the coastal crab centers, is now available in almost all large markets. Fresh crab meat is often offered in half and full pound containers. Most of the meat offered in this form has been blanched—that is, cooked in boiling water.

One advantage of buying precooked crab meat is that there is no waste the entire weight purchased is edible. Before serving, you should pick through the crab meat and remove any small bits of shell and tendons that remain.

Use freshly cooked crab meat very soon after you buy it to enjoy peak freshness. It will keep for about 3 days, if the crab meat remains refrigerated in the coldest part of the refrigerator.

Freshly cooked crab meat is offered in markets in the following forms:

LUMP CRAB MEAT: These are the large, white, most attractive pieces of meat from the backfin of the crab. These are the muscles that operated the swimming legs. Lump crab meat is the most expensive and highly regarded portion of the crab. Sometimes smaller pieces of lump meat are mixed with large pieces of flake meat and sold as backfin meat. Backfin meat will typically be a bit smaller than lump meat and should be correspondingly less expensive.

WHITE OR FLAKE CRAB MEAT: These are small pieces of the same sort white meat as the lump crab meat. It can be used anywhere the more expensive lump meat can be used, but each piece will be smaller.

CLAW MEAT: Claw meat is darker and a bit more coarsely textured than the lump, white, or flake meat. It comes from the large claws on the first set of crab legs. Since it is more coarsely textured, it can be frozen with greater success than the more delicately textured portion of the crab. Claw meat can replace white meat in any crab recipe, and many prefer it in soups and gumbos.

CRAB FINGERS: This is the claw meat when it has been left intact on the crab claw. Crab fingers are often used in crab meat cocktails so that a person can dip the crab meat in a sauce, then eat it holding on to the shell of the crab claw. Crab fingers are often sold precooked and make a handy and elegant appetizer. They also lend themselves to marinating and frying. Sometimes crab fingers are marketed as cocktail claws.

Frozen Crab Meat

Frozen crab meat is higher in quality than ever before and more readily available, because of improved freezing techniques, often involving freezing on board the fishing boat that harvested the crabs, and by a true revolution in transportation by wide-body jets. The result has been to push the boundaries of high quality frozen crab meat inland to cover virtually the whole United States.

The frozen crab meat most familiar to shoppers are crab legs, the frozen legs of the king, tanner, and other large walking crabs. These may be sold cut or split.

Another delicious crab available frozen is stone crab claws. Once cooked, stone crab claw meat may be frozen in the shell without significant loss of flavor. Kept frozen, stone crab claws retain their flavor for up to 6 months. When buying these claws, it is important to inspect them carefully. Select only those that are intact; do not purchase broken claws. An unbroken claw protects the meat inside, while a cracked claw can mean damaged meat. To defrost stone crab claws, thaw 12 to 18 hours in the refrigerator. Do not attempt to thaw this delicate meat under running water.

Freezing Crab Meat at Home

You can freeze crab meat in your home freezer, but there are some things you need to know.

First, never attempt to freeze whole crabs before cooking. A crab frozen whole and then thawed must be treated exactly like a dead crab, and thrown out. Some people get good results by cleaning a Dungeness crab and freezing the cleaned, uncooked crab in a block of ice. I think that better results are obtained by cooking fresh Dungeness crab meat and then freezing the cooked meat.

Attempting to freeze blue crab meat ends up with mixed results. Freezing toughens and dries crab meat, and blue crab meat is so finely textured that it suffers greater damage than more coarsely textured varieties.

Also, the longer the meat remains frozen, the more the taste and texture is harmed. I do not recommend attempting to freeze blue crab meat unless it is already cooked as an ingredient in crab cakes, soups, or other goodies. Frozen as part of a completed recipe, blue crab meat does not seem to deteriorate so badly.

To freeze Dungeness crab meat or any of the more coarsely textured meats:

1. If the crab is raw, cook the meat by steaming or boiling.
2. Immediately chill the crab and pick out the meat.
3. Pack the crab meat tightly in freezer proof bags.
4. Seal and label the bags, including the date.
5. Place in the coldest part of the freezer.

Stone crab claws may be frozen by following the technique above but do not crack the claws or remove the meat. The hard, thick claw of the stone crab protects the meat inside. The meat is easily removed after thawing.

Soft-shell crabs are among the best candidates for freezing. For instructions on freezing soft-shells, look in the section of this book immediately prior to the soft-shell crab recipes.

It is best to use home frozen crab meat within 1 month. Thaw the crab meat by holding in the refrigerator in the wrapper in which it was frozen. Do not attempt to thaw frozen crab meat by leaving at room temperature or holding under running water.

Pasteurized Crab Meat

Pasteurized crab meat is an excellent substitute for fresh. It must be stored in the refrigerator (not the freezer), where it can be held, unopened, for up to 6 months. In pasteurization the texture of the crab meat is not damaged as by freezing, nor is salt added as in canning. Thawing is not necessary. After the can is opened, pasteurized crab meat can be kept for the same time as freshly cooked meat. You can use it the same way you use fresh crab meat.

Pasteurized crab meat is made by packing cooked meat in cans that are hermetically sealed and immersed in a hot water bath. Color, taste, and texture are maintained. Pasteurization requires equipment and training beyond the home processor.

Canned Crab Meat

For many people, canned crab meat is a good substitute for fresh. Most canned crab meat has been picked by machines rather than by hand and is usually steamed Dungeness or king crab. Packers usually add salt, water, and citric or ascorbic acid to preserve color. I avoid canned crab meat containing EDTA or aluminum sulfate.

A significant advantage of canned crab meat is that it can be held, unopened, on the shelf for long periods without refrigeration. In addition, all of the meat is edible. There is no waste, but you should pick through the meat to remove any bone fragments or tendons that escaped the cannery.

Once opened, use canned crab as you would cooked fresh crab meat. After opening, the crab meat will spoil at the same rate as fresh crab meat and must be used immediately or kept under refrigeration.

In color, texture, and flavor, canned crab meat is less desirable than pasteurized. Unopened cans should never be placed in the freezer.

One of the less frequently used crabs, oyster crabs, are often sold in cans or sealed bottles. Typically, they are available only in large markets or speciality stores. Oyster crabs are small, less than an inch across, and are eaten whole. They are a prized ingredient in oyster stews and in delicately flavored garnishes and sauces. Oyster crabs are occasionally eaten raw.

To saute oyster crabs, place the crabs in a sieve or colander and rinse well in running water. Dip the crabs first in milk, and then in finely sifted flour. Shake off the extra flour and saute in clarified butter on low heat for 3 to 4 minutes. Lemon or lime mayonnaise is sometimes served with this dish.

Imitation Crab Meat

In the last few years, many food stores have begun to carry imitation crab meat. Sometimes this product is generically named and sometimes it is offered by brand. Many stores carry imitation crab meat labeled Surimi.

The Japanese pioneered the manufacture of imitation crab meat, using any number of varieties of mild-tasting whitefish such as pollock, cod, or whitefish, and some crab meat by-products. These are processed until their natural color and flavor are gone. Food colors, often including red dye, and flavorings are then added along with chemicals to simulate crab meat texture. The resulting products vary depending on the manufacturer. None of these products is crab meat, still the top end products offer good taste and texture; the bottom end stuff is not worth taking home, let alone buying.

Remember that no matter how imitation crab meat tastes or looks, nutritionally it is still the same as the fish from which it was made. In addition, salt may have been added during processing.

I do not recommend any of the imitation crab meat products. If you feel that you must use them you could put it in a casserole or one of the strongly flavored dishes. Personally, when crab meat is not available, I substitute fish.

Stretching Crab Meat

Sometimes you will find yourself with crab meat left over, but not with enough for dinner, and, most likely, you will have paid dear money for your crab meat. What to do? My solution is to prepare a dish where the available crab meat can be mixed with other ingredients without diminishing the taste of the meal. Six dishes lend themselves readily to light portions of crab meat:

- Creamed crab meat baked in shells or casseroles
- Crab cakes of crab meat blended with fillers
- Souffles with crab combinations
- Crab meat salads, or crab meat blended with dressings
- Spreads or dips using crab meat
- Soups or stews with crab meat and other ingredients

Another way to stretch crab meat is to add shrimp or another white-fleshed fish to the crab to make the correct amount of fish for the portions you need. But how much to add?

This chart will help. One serving of cooked crab meat is 1/4 pound, or 4 ounces. By reading down the chart under the column for the number of people you intend to serve, you can quickly see how many ounces you have per serving, and so how much you need to add. You can also measure how much crab meat you have, then read over the chart to determine how many ounces you have available.

For example, if you have 2 cups of crab meat available and 8 people to serve, you can read from the chart that each person will have 2 ounces of crab meat. This is less than the usual 4 ounce portion per person. This chart will tell you that you need an additional 2 ounces of fish, shrimp, or other fish for each of the 8 servings, or an extra pound of fish.

Cups	Pounds	Ounces		
		4 servings	6 servings	8 servings
1/2	1/4	1	3/4	1/2
1	1/2	2	1 1/2	1
1 1/2	3/4	3	2 1/4	1 1/2
2	1	4	3	2
2 1/2	1 1/4	5	3 3/4	2 1/2
3	1 1/2	6	4	3
3 1/2	1 3/4	7	5 1/4	3 1/2
4	2	8	6	4

Servings and Food Value

This chart and some simple math will provide a useful guideline for the amount of crab meat you need for a serving, depending on the market form you are buying.

For 1 Serving

cooked crab meat, blue crab claws	1/2 pound
cooked crab meat, picked crab meat	1/2 cup = 1/4 pound
blue crab, in shell, hard-shell	4 crabs, depending on size
blue crab, in shell, soft-shell	2-3 crabs, depending on size
Dungeness crab, in shell	1/2 crab
king crab, frozen leg sections	1/5 pound
oyster crab, in shell	1/8 pound
rock crab, in shell	4-6 crabs, depending on size
stone crab claws	3-4 claws, depending on size

Food Value of Crab Meat

Since crab meat is a natural rather than synthetic food, its composition varies. The following information is for 100 grams (almost 4 ounces) of freshly cooked crab. Canned crab meat may be different depending on the method of processing used; it will almost certainly have more sodium and may have more calories. Figures may vary slightly for different species of crabs. Figures cited are from government and industry sources.

Calories	93.0
Total Fat	2.59% of the U.S. Recommended Daily Allowance
Composition	
Ascorbic Acid	2.0 mg
Calcium	32.0 mg
Carbohydrates	.5 g
Cholesterol (king)	70.0 mg
Cholesterol (blue)	113.0 mg
Fat	1.9 g
Iron	.8 mg
Niacin	2.8 mg
Phosphorous	175.0 mg
Protein	17.3 g
Riboflavin	.08 mg
Sodium (king)	1,216.0 mg
Sodium (blue)	316.0 mg
Thiamin	.160 mg
Vitamin A	2,170 IU
Magnesium	34.0 mg
Water	78.5%

Harvesting from the Sea

Crabbing is fun and easy. It requires almost no skill. Even a person with no experience can expect good success catching crabs. Children especially enjoy it, and the thrill on youngsters' faces when they pull a crab in with their net is indescribable.

Fishing Regulations

There are two kinds of crab seasons: the legal season and the time of year when the life cycle of the crab provides the best catch. The legal season is easiest to determine: simply contact the fish and game authorities in the area you plan to fish. They can tell you when you can crab, how many you can take, and the legal size limits, and if a fishing license is necessary.

Crabbing seasons and catch limits are regulated by states, so laws are likely to vary. You may be pleasantly surprised to learn that in many areas amateur catches of certain crab species may be taken without any restrictions on size or number. When some crabs are legal but others not, it is wise to have at least some knowledge of what the various species look like.

One regulation exists in almost all states: it is a violation to keep egg-bearing females. These protected crabs can be recognized by a cluster of bright orange eggs, or roe on the crab's underside.

There is a recurring problem you should avoid. Sometimes people begin fishing in a lonely spot and after a bit their enthusiasm outpaces their devotion to the law. Before temptation overcomes virtue, remember that limits on the type, size, sex, or amount of crabs we may take do not exist for the benefit of the crabs. They are in place for our benefit, so that there will be plenty of fully grown crabs next year, the year after, and on into the next generation. In addition, many local laws have more bite than a crab's claw. If you are going to cheat, bring plenty of money.

While you are checking for local fishing regulations, you should also check with local authorities to see if the area is safe and free of pollutants. Unfortunately, this simple precaution is becoming more important as time goes by.

I do not crab in waters near heavily industrialized areas or where dumping of chemicals is frequent or notorious. Crabs are bottom feeders and, what is worse from the standpoint of catching a contaminated crab, the little rascals are mobile. Unlike many fin fish, there is no indication that crabs are territorial. A crab may eat something in a contaminated area, then thoughtlessly scurry someplace else for you to catch him. Avoiding the effects of pollution is tricky enough business without itinerant crabs making it worse. So play it safe and crab only in waters you are reasonably sure are free (and far) from sources of pollution. It takes only one call to your local heath department or fish and game department.

Stalking the Crab

There is a wide range of estimates of the best season and time of day to go crabbing, but the most experienced crabbing hands seem to agree on two points. Crabs tend to move inshore and take bait more readily during the summer months. This belief is firmly rooted in the life cycle of the crab and relates to the crab molting season. Beginning in early spring and continuing into fall crabs move into the sun-warmed shallow waters near shore. During this time crabs eat more, grow faster, and shed their hard, outer shells to accommodate their growth. It is while they are inshore in larger numbers, all hungrily scurrying around looking for food that a crab is most likely to find your bait and be caught.

Crabs are unreliable and apt to turn up when and where you least expect them. Hard by this information is a piece of advice really worth taking to heart: when you go crabbing, the best thing to do is to seek advice from people who are familiar with local conditions.

If I write that crabs prefer slow moving waters with gentle tides, as they usually do, someone is sure to haul in a record catch in an area with swiftly moving tides. And as I write that crabs are more likely to be caught during midday, they will be jumping into your net at sundown. In other words, crabs have a generous streak of unpredictability. They are where you find them, which is not necessarily where you may expect them.

I think that the best thing to do before crabbing in a unfamiliar area is visit several of the local bait shops. You can ask where the good crabbing spots are. You can find out the time of day that the crabs are most plentiful. The point is that in a coastal community where there is any crabbing at all, a brief search will turn up a wealth of information, and you should not be shy about asking.

If you are going travel to some distance, a trip to the local library might be worthwhile. Look in the telephone book yellow page section covering the area you will be visiting and check for bait shops. A few calls will give you some useful information.

Crabbing Equipment

Unlike many sports, crab fishing requires almost no equipment, and what you do need is cheap. You need (1) a line, net, or trap to get the crabs from the water onto the land, (2) a heavy glove or pair of tongs to catch the crabs once you have landed them, and (3) a container to hold the crabs until you clean or cook them.

The most basic device to catch crabs is the baited string. This method of fishing must have been familiar to our earliest ancestors, but it is just as good today and many people use it. To fish this way, tie a chicken neck, slice of salt pork, or a fish head (the frowsier the better) on the end of a thick line. Add a weight to pull the bait to the bottom. Drop the bait in the water, let it settle, and wait.

When a crab takes your bait, he may or may not signal you with a gentle tug on the line. If you do not feel a pull on the line, wait about 15 minutes, then slowly draw the line up as smoothly and carefully as your excitement will allow. Avoid jerks or fast moves that might cause the crab to drop the bait and scurry off. When the bait is just below the surface, check the line for a crab. If you see that you have a crab clinging to the bait, slip a dip net underneath him and bring him in. If you have never fished for crabs you may think this method is too simple to catch anything, but crabs are more stubborn than smart and most will hold onto the bait all the way to the surface.

Another way to catch crabs is to wade into relatively clear water with a dip net, scooping up crabs as you go. Personally, I think that this is the hardest way, for all its seeming simplicity. In the first place, many of the more active crabs will run away from a dip net. In the second, it is far too easy to lose your footing while you are distracted by the search for crabs. Worse still, you may hurt yourself on some of the man-made garbage that people throw all too readily into the sea. And third, when you crab this way, you are far more exposed to the elements than while fishing by other methods. Often it is just too hot or too cold to think of going wading.

I use traps. They give much better results than a baited string and are even easier to use. They are inexpensive and almost never wear out. Traps can be used from boats and piers. They can be dropped into the water

To Catch a Crab

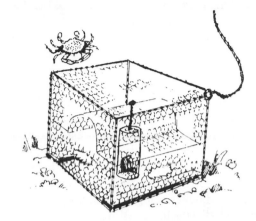

Crab Ring— it is lowered into the water so it lays flat, then picked up trapping the crabs inside. It is often used from a dock or boat because the crab ring is usually drawn straight out of the water.

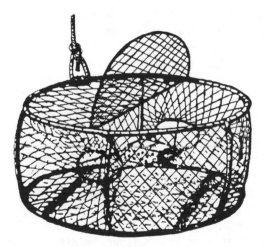

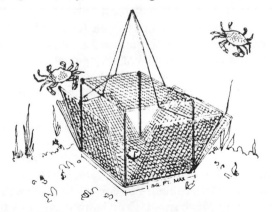

Crab Trap—when the dropline is pulled, the sides are pulled up trapping the crabs inside.

Crab Pots— usually made out of chicken wire and can be almost any shape that will sit on the bottom. Crab pots are larger than rings or pyramid traps and can be left unattended all day if necessary. They may be many times larger than attended traps. I have seen crab pots the size of an office desk.

vertically and do not involve throwing or casting which is likely to tangle a net while it is being dragged back.

One type of trap, the easiest to use and cheapest to buy, is called a crab ring. A crab ring is made of two metal loops, one larger than the other. The trap has fish net sides and a fish net bottom; the top is completely open. In appearance, a crab ring is something like a basketball goal with a bottom in it. It looks a bit like a collapsible bucket made of fish net.

A crab trap uses the same bait as a baited string. Tie the bait securely inside the smaller of the two metal loops. Lower the crab ring to the sea bottom by a dropline. The crab ring is designed so that when it is rests on the bottom, it lays flat. After about 15 minutes, raise the trap. Three or four lines go from the top loop to the dropline, attached so that when the dropline is lifted, the trap will lift out of the water like a bucket, trapping inside any crabs feasting on the bait. Unlike the baited string, a crab ring should be pulled to the surface quickly; the pressure of the water against the crabs will help hold them in the trap. When you use a crab ring, you do not need a separate dip net, as with the baited string.

Another crab trap, similar in principle to the crab ring, is made entirely of metal. It is shaped like a miniature pyramid. The sides of the pyramid are hinged so that the trap lies flat when it rests on the sea bottom. A dropline passes through a ring at the apex of the pyramid. When the line is pulled, it draws up the sides on the pyramid to form a cage. The chief advantage of this trap is that no openings are left through which the crab can escape, unlike the open-topped ring trap. Metal pyramid traps are more expensive than crab rings and are probably worth the price if you intend to do a lot of crabbing over a long period of time. Metal pyramid traps probably allow fewer crabs to escape. In addition, a metal trap will last more or less indefinitely.

A third type of crab trap is used by really serious crabbers or by small commercial operators. These traps are larger, heavier, and left for longer periods between checking. Often these traps are attached to floats and dropped from boats. Typically, traps of this type are left for several hours between inspection. In some states they are subject to different regulation than traps designed for amateur use. Traps of this sort may also be referred to as crab pots.

The crab pot is essentially a box, usually made of chicken wire on a wooden or metal frame. It has an entrance that is similar to fish traps constructed by primitive men. These traps have an opening that is wide and easy for the crab to find from the sea side, but narrow and difficult to find once the crab is inside. From the crab's point of view, it is a bit like walking through a funnel. Often holes are placed along the walls of the trap large enough to allow undersize crabs to escape, but small enough to keep the legal catch securely penned.

My first experience crabbing was with one of these traps. My guide claimed he knew what he was doing, so I followed his lead. Early one morning we loaded the trap in the trunk of his car. We drove to a likely looking marshy area. After tying a number of chicken necks in the trap, we put on wading boots and carried the trap into the water. We put the trap up against a concrete post and tied it in place. We got into the car and drove away. So far, everything had gone according to plans.

By late afternoon things had changed. The temperature had fallen and the smell of rain was in the air. We returned to retrieve the crab pot. By now the rain had started. It was cold and the wind was blowing. We put our wading boots back on and walked to the concrete anchor post.

The crab pot was gone. Sloshing around knee deep in saltwater we circled to look for it. While I sincerely and fluently expressed my hopes for the final resting place of all crabs, my companion allowed as how it could be worse. I was in the middle of asking how, when a wave broke over the top of my wading boots and water poured in. To add insult to injury, after finding the crab pot and dragging it to shore, our catch was meager. All things considered, the experience went a long way toward explaining to me where crabbing got its name.

This experience helps to point out the advantages of a crab ring. If it gets cold or rainy, you can leave without leaving your trap behind. You don't have to get wet. And you get immediate results. You know right away if you are going to catch crabs or if you need to find a better location.

Holding the Crab

So you've caught one of the little fellows—now what? Let's imagine that you have a hard-shell blue crab about 7 inches wide. He is sitting in the bottom of your crab ring or dip net glowering at you. The crab is definitely unhappy about having been pulled from the water and seems like the sort to hold a grudge. From time to time he waves a pair of unfriendly looking claws in your direction. You are pretty sure that he will scamper away at the first opportunity. What do you do?

You must first get the crab out of the crab ring or dip net, and then if you don't cook your catch on the spot, you must keep him alive for later. It is no good catching the crab if you handle him so roughly that you kill him and have to throw him away.

Now, back to the crab glowering at you from the crab ring. How do you get him out and into whatever container you intend to keep him? The easy way is just to turn the crab ring upside down over your container, or over a rapidly boiling pot, if you are cooking your catch.

Or you can move the crab safely from the trap to your holding container, wearing a heavy glove. Just pick him up. The blue crab's claws may look frightening, and they can give you a startling nip if you are not careful, but they are harmless to a heavily gloved hand. If you have caught a stone crab, do not pick the crab up so cavalierly. The stone crab has remarkably powerful pincers capable of giving a painful injury. Always use extreme care when handling them.

The old fashioned way to catch a crab (and this takes either practice or courage) is to use that old standby: slip up on him from behind. Crabs are not very bright. Divert the crab's attention by waving one hand just out of his reach, then grab him from behind with your other. He will not be able to reach backward with his claws and will be helpless. Personally, I favor a compound technique. I use a heavy glove and slip up on him from behind, too.

A set of tongs is often useful. Most well-stocked kitchens have a suitable pair. The same tongs will also serve when you are handling the crabs after cooking. I think that fireplace tongs are really too large to be manageable. They also pose a risk that your crabs will be killed in handling.

If, while you are handling your crab catch, a crab loses a leg or claw, do not feel guilty; you just witnessed a very natural process. One of the defensive mechanisms of the crab is the ability to escape predators by shedding its legs. Crabs have the ability to cast off their injured or trapped legs, including their claws. This is a reflex action called autotomy. In the sea a new, regenerated leg or claw is grown, and the process can be repeated 3 or 4 times for each appendage.

Some people carry clippers and snip off one of the claws from each pair of pincers After this has been done, the crab is totally harmless. Crabs that have been declawed in this manner are also less able to injure other crabs held in the same container.

Bringing Them Back Alive

Crabs need to remain damp and cool. One of the handiest ways to keep crabs is in a burlap bag moistened with sea water. Continue to moisten the bag as it dries out. If you use a bag as a container, be sure to tie the top securely or the crabs will crawl out. If you are crabbing from a boat or pier, the bag can be tied to the side and kept in the water. When you need to get the crabs out, turn the bag inside out.

You can keep crabs in a box, bucket, or basket, almost anything with a lid. You can cover the crabs with a moistened bag covered with any sort of lid, or, as folks do in Louisiana, with damp Spanish moss. I like to keep crabs in a plastic foam ice chest. Chests of this type are cheap, readily available, and easy to clean. They have a flat bottom and a closely fitted lid. The crabs will keep well if you start with a shallow layer of ice.

People who crab from boats equipped with an aerated well keep crabs quite satisfactorily. They do not attempt to keep crabs in still water. The oxygen supply in still water is limited and the crabs will soon die of suffocation. Without an aeration chamber, it is much better to keep crabs in the open air.

Do not hesitate to pack the crabs somewhat tightly. Crabs packed loosely will tend to fight and injure or kill one another. As long as the crabs are kept damp and cool they should travel perfectly well in close quarters.

Remember that however you handle or move your crabs, you must discard any that have died before you cook your catch. If you have stored your crabs on ice, inactive crabs should be examined with special care. Live crabs should be active, but, after sitting on ice for a while, even a healthy crab may show little movement. To be absolutely sure, check for eye movement. If you are in doubt, throw the crab away. Do not cook dead ones.

All about Soft-Shell Crabs

Catching Soft-Shell Crabs

Soft-shell crabs comprise less than 3 percent of the total crab catch, but they are prized beyond compare. Broiled, grilled, and sauteed soft-shell crabs are an increasingly popular American treat. Some people hold that there is no finer dish available in the United States than a plate of well-prepared soft-shell crabs. Unlike the hard-shell crab from which cooked meat is picked and the rest of the crab discarded, soft-shell crabs are entirely edible.

It is very important to buy fresh soft-shell crabs, for they are an inherently fragile food that can be spoiled by ill handling. If you are lucky enough to live in a crabbing area, the best way to ensure freshness is to catch them yourself. If you do, there are some things you need to know.

A soft-shell crab is any crab that has shed its hard, outer shell in preparation for a new one, a process that is part of the life cycle of all true crabs. I write about blue soft-shell crabs because this is a cookbook, and soft-shell blue crabs are the only ones you are ever likely to see at table or in the market. Dungeness soft-shells are protected by law and so are not available in markets. Stone crabs are protected in both hard- and soft-shell. Any of the deep-water crabs such as king, tanner, or snow crabs that are caught without their hard shells are presumably either thrown back into the sea or processed along with the others. I do not know of any commercially viable markets for soft-shell crabs in any of the minor species, although from time to time they may be caught in water they frequent.

The first thing you must know about catching soft-shell crabs is that fishing regulations for taking soft-shell crabs may be different from the regulations for taking hard-shell crabs of the same variety. In addition, the regulations may vary among local areas. Do not assume that fishing laws treat hard- and soft-shell crabs equally. You should always check local fishing laws before dropping your net or trap. Assuming that soft-shell catches are legal where you intend to go crabbing, what do you do? And just what is a soft-shell anyway?

All true crabs are exoskelites, that is, with external skeletons commonly referred to as shells. These outer shells must be shed in order for the crab to grow. Beginning from hatching size of about 1/25th of an inch, crabs shed their shells many times during their life cycle. For instance, in the 2-year life of the blue crab, a crab grows a new shell up to 25 times, mostly during the first year of life when it achieves almost all its adult growth. Each time that the crab sheds its shell, it increases its size by about one-third.

During the cold winter months most crabs are relatively dormant and eat sparingly. Typically they show little growth and seldom require new shells. But with the coming of warmer weather in late spring, crabs begin to eat in a serious way. Their feeding continues during the summer and into early fall. It is during this time the crab grows most rapidly and the old shell begins to pinch around the edges. The crab's shell needs to be replaced with a roomier model, just like a fat person needing a new pair of pants.

When the crab's body begins to get too big for its shell, a new soft skeleton will form underneath the old. The old hard shell will break apart and be cast off. The soft, new shell will now be the only protection the crab has.

Immediately after shedding, the crab takes in excess water and begins to swell. After about 2 hours, and while the crab is still enlarged with extra water, the soft shell will begin to harden. The purpose of the extra water is to bloat the crab so that the hard shell will form, leaving extra room in which the crab will grow. If swelling did not occur, the new shell, formed as it was underneath the old one, would actually be smaller than the one that was cast off, leaving the crab in an awful predicament.

For the next 2 days the hardening will continue, after which the soft shell will have completed its transformation into the familiar armored cover the crab needs to survive.

During the hardening process, the crab is extremely vulnerable to attack. Crabs inhabit waters that teem with all sorts of hungry creatures, including other crabs. This host of predators, of which man is among the least efficient, knows that soft-shell crabs are tasty treats. If crabs did not have some defense, few soft-shells would survive.

Crabs become very inactive while they have soft shells. Since most predators are attracted to movement, the less active a soft-shell is, the better it is equipped to survive this perilous time. In addition, the less active a soft-shell is, the more likely the crab is to avoid fatal accidents while it is inadequately protected.

A second natural defense is to hide in any brush or vegetation available. Combining the two defenses, it is easy to see how a crab lying very still in a pile of underwater brush would escape the wrong sort of attention from passing predators. Once the crab's shell has hardened, these two defensive traits disappear, and the crab emerges its old, active self with all its accustomed habits.

The defensive reactions of the soft-shells suggests a strategy for catching them. Experienced hunters adapt themselves to the habits of their prey, and soft-shell fishermen are not exceptions. During the soft-shell season, fishermen take brush and tie lines and floats to their brush and drop it into the shallow, sluggish water favored by crabs.

To a soft-shell crab, this brush seems an ideal hiding place. Actually it is a trap. After the brush has been in the water long enough to attract soft-shells looking for shelter, the brush is pulled up, soft-shell crabs and all. In this case, the soft-shell crab's inactivity works against him, since a more active crab would be more likely to drop from the brush back into the water.

But most soft-shell crabs are not caught by dropping brush in water. In fact, most are caught neither during the two hours before hardening begins nor even during the two days before hardening is complete. Most soft-shell crabs are caught before their shells become soft, that is, before molting begins.

The real skill in catching soft-shells lies in having a practiced eye to spot the signs of a hard-shell crab about to molt. Crabbers carefully examine their catches for the signs that they have caught one of these little treasures, for they are a sure way to raise the value of their catch. Peelers—crabs ready to shed their skins—can be recognized by a thin pink line that appears on the fourth pair of legs. They also develop a particular scarlet color on one of their claws. If you do not know what to look for, or where, you are likely to miss it, for it is a skill that must be acquired.

Once caught, these special crabs are typically placed in floating cribs or tanks until they have molted, and many a lad has begun his career as a crabber carefully watching the tanks for newly shed crabs. Since the new soft-shells are vulnerable to attack even while in the shedding tanks, the new soft-shell crab must be removed at once from the tank.

The best areas to fish for soft-shell crabs are shallow grass beds, rocks, and mud flats. Since soft-shells are less active, they can be caught more successfully wading with a dip net. The relative inactivity of soft-shells makes it unlikely that traps used for hard-shell crabs will yield much success.

If you catch a crab that has incompletely shed its shell, holding him in a bucket of water will usually complete the molting. After shedding is complete, remove the soft-shell from the water immediately. Hardening of the shell stops when the crab is out of water, and the softer the shell of the crab is, the better it is for your table.

Buying Soft-Shell Crabs

Soft-shell crabs may be purchased alive, freshly cleaned, or frozen. Freshness is important when selecting most foods, but it is especially important for soft-shells. Soft-shells are inherently fragile and subject to spoilage from rough handling or from being kept too long.

After a crab has shed its shell, the new shell begins to harden very rapidly, so soft-shells must be eaten or frozen quickly. A soft-shell is at its peak immediately after shedding. After that point, time runs against quality.

Preparing Soft-Shell Crabs for Cooking

1. Use scissors to cut off the front part of the crab's head in back of the eyes, about 1/2 inch into the leading edge of the crab.

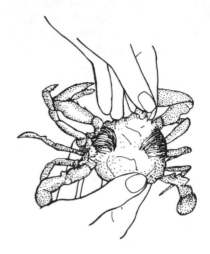

2. With scissors or fingers, remove and discard the sand bag from behind the crab's mouth.

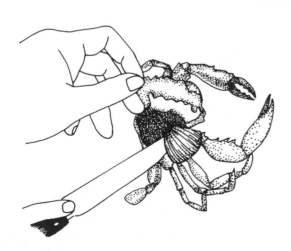

3. Lift the shell at each of the pointed ends. Remove and discard the white gill sacks from each side of the crab.

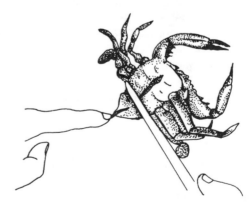

4. Gently pull the apron from the bottom rear of the crab. The intestinal vein should pull away with the apron. Discard. Do not worry about further cleaning the intestinal tract. Wash crab in cold, salted water.

Even the miracles of modern transportation have been unable to move fresh soft-shells quickly enough to avoid the rapid hardening of the shell. After only two hours the new shell begins to harden, and in two days the hardening is complete. If you live near an area where fresh soft-shells are offered, you are fortunate.

The finest flavor and freshness will be obtained from buying soft-shells alive at market and cleaning them yourself immediately before cooking. When you shop for live soft-shells, look for movement, particularly around the eyes and mouth. A soft-shell is in a weak, inactive stage of its life cycle. In addition, if the soft-shell has been refrigerated, this will further slow up its movement. You should never buy a soft-shell or any other crab that exhibits no movement, for it is almost surely dead, not suitable for cooking.

Freshly cleaned soft-shells are a close second to live soft-shells for flavor, if you cook them soon after purchasing. Soft-shell crabs lose the peak of flavor and juiciness soon after cleaning and dressing. If you cannot cook the crabs quickly, it is better to purchase them alive or frozen.

When buying freshly cleaned soft-shells, first select crabs that are alive in the store and cleaned while you wait, for these will be the most fresh

If only precleaned soft-shells are available, ask how long the crab has been in the fishmonger's case. Avoid crabs more than two days old. If you are buying a precleaned crab, look for crabs with a clean, ammonia-free smell. If the crab is tightly enclosed in a plastic wrap container, ask to have the container opened to allow you to smell for freshness. No reputable fishmonger will resent your interest in the quality of his merchandise; your satisfaction is his best guarantee of a return sale.

Soft-shell crabs may be cleaned and then frozen. Although the quality of frozen soft-shell crabs may be excellent, they should be your last choice if live or freshly cleaned crabs are available. Often merchants handling both fresh and frozen soft-shell crabs will save their freshly cleaned soft-shells until the last possible moment, then prolong their shelf-life by offering them for sale frozen. If your merchant is careful, there is nothing wrong with this practice which benefits consumers by reducing overall waste and thereby reducing prices. Unfortu-nately, if a fishmonger waits too late to freeze the cleaned crab, you could get a crab at the very end of its shelf-life, or beyond. There is very little way to tell ahead of time, except by knowing your fishmonger and his reputation for quality, so choose live or freshly cleaned crabs when possible.

When you do buy frozen soft-shells, you should select crabs that are well wrapped and solidly frozen. If the date of freezing is available, choose the most recently dated crabs. In no case select crabs more than 6 months old, the extreme range of their useful life.

Although frozen soft-shells may be prepared in all the ways fresh soft-shells may be cooked, freezing takes some of the natural juiciness from the fresh crab. For this reason, many people feel that frozen soft-shells are best fried, since frying crisps the crabs and does not require juiciness.

Market Grades/Sizes

Soft-shell crabs are graded by size rather than quality. Size grading, which may vary somewhat from market to market, is defined by the width of the crab across the widest part of the shell. The size grades are:

Whale	over 5.5 inches
Jumbo	5 to 5.5 inches
Prime	4.5 to 5 inches
Hotel	4 to 4.5 inches
Medium	3.5 to 4 inches

There is almost no market interest in soft-shell crabs below 3.5 inches, and crabs below this size are not graded.

Cleaning Soft-Shell Crabs

The easiest way to clean a soft-shell crab is to ask the fishmonger to do it for you when you buy it. Most fish markets offer this service to their customers. But do not have the crab cleaned at market unless you are going to cook the crab immediately. Natural juiciness and flavor suffer very quickly once the crab has been cleaned.

If you are going to clean your crabs yourself, store the soft-shells you have captured or bought in the refrigerator between moist towels or newspapers. A shallow box, loosely covered or a paper grocery bag makes a good container. The crabs will not move about or crawl through your refrigerator. They will live for about a day, but the longer you keep them the more likely they will die. To clean a soft-shell crab:

1. Rinse the live crab under running water several times.

2. Kill the crab by sticking a small, sharp knife into the body between the eyes.

3. Use scissors to cut off the front part of the crab's head in back of the eyes, about 1/2 inch into the leading edge of the crab.

4. With the scissors or fingers, remove and discard the sand bag from behind the crab's mouth.

5. Lift the shell at each of the pointed ends. Remove and discard the white gill sacks from each side of the crab.

6. If the crab is retaining moisture from the shedding of its hard shell, pierce the underbelly several times with a small sharp knife and allow the water to drain.

7. Gently pull the apron from the bottom rear of the crab. The intestinal vein should pull away with the apron. Discard. Do not worry about further cleaning the intestinal tract. For several days prior to molting crabs do not eat. The digestive tract of the crab will be clean and empty.

8. Wash the crab in cold salted water and dry on absorbent paper.

Keeping Soft-Shell Crabs

If you do not choose to cook your cleaned crab immediately, seal the crab tightly in plastic wrap and refrigerate immediately. It will keep for about 2 days. Soft-shells must be cleaned before freezing.

If you want to freeze the crab, it will keep for up to 6 months if stored in the coldest part of the freezer. To prepare the crab for freezing, simply wrap the cleaned crab tightly in plastic wrap, one crab to a container to minimize the air space.

To thaw frozen soft-shells, place the crabs in a pan of cool water in the refrigerator. Do not attempt to thaw crabs in hot water or the taste and texture of the crab will suffer.

Appetizers

Crab Cocktail

This is an old favorite that is sure to please. Served with crackers or lightly buttered garlic toast, it is the perfect beginning to an elegant meal. The more flavorful the ketchup you use in this sauce, the better the results.

1 cup ketchup
1 tablespoon prepared horseradish
2 teaspoons worcestershire sauce
1 teaspoon white pepper
1 teaspoon black pepper
1 teaspoon salt
1/2 teaspoon garlic powder
1 teaspoon onion powder

Lettuce or spinach leaves to line the serving cup or dish

3 cups (1 1/2 pounds) lump crab meat
1 1/2 cups finely chopped green bell pepper
1 1/2 cups finely chopped celery

To make the cocktail sauce, combine the ingredients and stir to mix. Chill for at least 1 hour.

To assemble the crab cocktail, line the serving dish with lettuce or spinach leaves. Stir the crab meat, green pepper, and celery together. Stir gently, so that the large lumps of crab meat are not broken. Heap the crab meat mixture on the greens. Spoon the cocktail sauce over the salad. Serve chilled.

Yield: 12 servings

Smoked Crab Log

Annette Reddell Hegen with the Texas A&M Marine Advisory Service is one of the Texas Gulf coast's most outstanding cooks. She gave me this recipe for crab with cream cheese log. This is a party-time treat with a special smoky flavor not usually associated with crab meat. It is easy to prepare this ahead and chill until needed.

8 ounces cream cheese, softened
1 tablespoon fresh lemon juice
2 teaspoons grated onion
2 teaspoons prepared horseradish
1 teaspoon liquid smoke
1/4 teaspoon salt
2 cups (1 pound) crab meat
1/2 cup chopped pecans
2 tablespoons chopped fresh parsley

Mash together the softened cream cheese, lemon juice, onion, horseradish, liquid smoke, and salt. Stir in the crab meat and mix thoroughly. Chill the mixture for several hours.

Turn the crab meat mixture onto waxed paper and shape into a log roll. Stir together the pecans and parsley. Roll the crab meat log in the nut mixture until lightly and evenly coated. Serve chilled with salted nuts and an assortment of crackers.

Yield: about 30 hors d'oeuvres

Cream Cheese— Crab Spread-Dip

The Pickapeppa Sauce is Jamaican in origin, with a distinctive flavor that goes especially well with this blend of ingredients. Most large grocery stores now stock Pickapeppa Sauce but, if yours does not, it is worth calling around for a source. If you absolutely cannot obtain it, substitute worcestershire sauce.

8 ounces cream cheese
1/4 cup milk
1/4 cup celery, finely chopped
1 tablespoon lime juice
2 teaspoons Pickapeppa Sauce
1 clove finely chopped garlic
1/8 teaspoon salt
1/4 teaspoon pepper blend (see page 131)
1 cup (1/2 pound) crab meat

Beat the cream cheese and the milk together. Add the rest of the ingredients. Stir to combine. Gently fold in the crab meat. Serve chilled with buttered toast triangles.

Yield: 1 1/2 cups

Crab Meat Spread-Dip

This spread has a more traditional flavor than the preceding recipe. I serve it with crackers as well as with toast spread with just a hint of garlic butter. It is also a knockout dip, sure to keep people standing around the buffet table. When you make this, make plenty!

2 tablespoons mayonnaise
1 teaspoon olive oil, if using bottled mayonnaise
1/2 cup (1/4 pound) crab meat
1 teaspoon lemon juice
2 teaspoons chopped capers
2 teaspoons finely chopped parsley
1/8 teaspoon Tabasco

If you are using bottled mayonnaise, place the mayonnaise in a glass or stainless steel mixing bowl. Add the olive oil in a fine stream, stirring constantly. Continue to stir until the oil is thoroughly blended into the mayonnaise.

Add the remaining ingredients and mix thoroughly. Refrigerate until well chilled and serve.

Yield: about 30 hors d'oeuvres

Crab Mousse ✓

The mango chutney in this mousse adds just the right touch of flavor. If you do not employ a bit of chutney in your cooking, this will be a pleasing surprise. Chutney has been served at Hindu tables for over 4,000 years. The word itself comes from the Hindu word for appetizer. Most mango chutneys include—in addition to mangos—ginger, lime, vinegar, pepper, and assorted spices.

1 tablespoon gelatin
3 tablespoons warm water
3 tablespoons heavy cream, warmed
2 cups (1 pound) crab meat
2 teaspoons chopped fresh parsley
1 teaspoon dried chives
1 tablespoon mango chutney
1 tablespoon lime juice
1/2 pint cream, whipped
Oil to coat mold
Lettuce leaves

To make the mousse, dissolve the gelatin in warm water, stirring gently. When the gelatin is fully dissolved, blend in the warm cream.

Reserving the whipped cream, combine the gelatin mix with the remaining ingredients. When the mixture begins to set, fold in the whipped cream and pour the mixture into an oiled mold.

Chill until firm, then turn the mousse out of the mold. Serve chilled, on a bed of lettuce leaves.

Yield: 4 servings

Crab Meat and Avocado Mousse

Josh Robinson, a friend and gourmet chef, created this dish after a trip to Santa Barbara, California. Josh, a devoted mousse freak, thinks this is the best crab mousse he has ever tasted.

3/4 ounces gelatin
1/4 cup hot water
3 large avocados, cut in quarters, peeled and stoned
2 tablespoons mayonnaise
1 teaspoon lime juice
1/2 teaspoon salt
1/4 teaspoon white pepper
3 green onions, tops included, finely chopped
2 stalks of celery, leaves included, finely chopped
1/2 cup heavy cream
1/2 cup (1/4 pound) crab meat
Oil to coat mold
Lettuce leaves

Dissolve the gelatin in the hot water. Set aside. Combine the avocados, mayonnaise, lime juice, salt, pepper, onions, celery, and dissolved gelatin in an electric blender and whirl for 30 seconds until the mixture is a smooth puree.

In a large bowl, combine the crab meat and cream. Stir until thoroughly combined. Gently stir together the mixture from the blender and the mixture from the bowl.

Lightly grease a mold with avocado oil or any light oil. Pour the crab and avocado mixture into the mold. Chill for 4 hours.

To remove the mousse from the mold, loosen the mixture from the mold with a knife with a thin, sharp blade. Set the bottom of the mold in very hot water. Turn the mold upside down in a plate. The mousse should slide out into the plate. Serve chilled, on a bed of lettuce leaves.

Yield: 6 servings

Southern Crab Puffs

I am always glad to have dishes that can be made ahead and held ready for serving. This elegant crab puff recipe came from New Orleans and certainly is a fine representative of the cosmopolitan tastes of the Crescent City.

1/4 cup mayonnaise
2 teaspoons olive oil, if using bottled mayonnaise
6 ounces cream cheese, softened
2 cups (1 pound) crab meat
1 1/2 cups ground pecans
2 tablespoon mango chutney
1 teaspoon salt
1 teaspoon curry powder
1 cup shredded dried coconut

If you are using bottled mayonnaise, place the mayonnaise in a glass or stainless steel mixing bowl. Add the olive oil in a fine stream, stirring constantly. Continue to stir until the oil is thoroughly blended into the mayonnaise.

Combine the cream cheese with the mayonnaise. Add the remaining ingredients, except for the shredded coconut. Mix thoroughly, and roll into pecan-size balls. Roll the crab puffs in the coconut and serve chilled.

Yield: about 30 hors d'oeuvres

Marinated Crab Claws

Marinated crab claws are a simple, flavorful treat that is always welcome at my table. I suppose there are as many marinade recipes as there are leaves on the trees, but this one works well for me. I have come back to it again and again, sometimes adding ingredients, sometimes taking them away, but never far from the recipe you see here. As always, use fresh herbs if possible. The quantities I give here are for fresh herbs.

1 1/2 cups olive oil
6 tablespoons white wine vinegar
1 lime, juiced
2 cloves minced garlic
1/2 tablespoon Tabasco
2 teaspoons fresh oregano
2 teaspoons fresh basil
2 teaspoons fresh chopped parsley
1 teaspoon fresh oregano
1 teaspoon pepper blend (see page 131)
1/2 teaspoon salt
1/4 teaspoon dried dill

24 cooked crab claws from blue, Dungeness, or stone crab

To prepare the marinade, combine the ingredients and stir until thoroughly blended.

To marinate the crab claws, place the claws in the bottom of a shallow dish. Cover with the marinade, cover, and refrigerate overnight.

To serve the crab claws, drain and reserve the marinade. Arrange the crab claws on a serving plate. Serve the marinade as a dipping sauce for the claws.

Yield: 4 servings blue or Dungeness crab claws; 12 servings stone crab claws

Ann Richards' Hot Crab Dip

Ann Richards gave me this recipe just before she was inaugurated as governor of Texas. She allowed as how she was especially anxious to share this dish since it was unlikely she would be spending much time in the kitchen for the next four years and wanted other people to enjoy this for her. The governor serves this with crackers or melba toast. She said that if you are serving a large crowd, layer the almonds and chips halfway as well as on top. The governor went on to say that her favorite bait for crabs is chicken necks. They are bony and stay on the string and the crabs seem to hang on longer during the pull to shore.

8 ounces cream cheese
1 tablespoon milk
1 cup (1/2 pound) crab meat
2 tablespoons finely chopped onion
1/2 tablespoon salt
Dash of pepper
1/2 cup slivered almonds
1/4 cup crumbled potato chips

Preheat the oven to 350 degrees F. Blend the cream cheese and milk. Combine this mixture with crab meat, onion, salt, and pepper. Mix well and spoon into an oven-proof baking dish.

In a separate bowl, mix the slivered almonds and a few crumbled potato chips. Sprinkle this mixture over the top of the cream cheese and crab meat.

Bake the crab dip for 15 minutes. Serve hot.

Yield: about 30 hors d'oeuvres

Baked Crab Balls

These crab balls have a rich taste accented with the pleasant tang of lime. Like many of the appetizers I favor, these bite-size treats are as good chilled as they are hot. You can also refrigerate them until you are ready to pop them in the oven. It is best to let them come to room temperature before you bake them.

4 tablespoons butter, melted
3 cups (1 1/2 pounds) crab meat
3 cups fresh bread crumbs (about 4 slices)
1 cup ketchup
3 tablespoons lime juice
1 tablespoon finely chopped parsley
1 tablespoon fresh tarragon
1/2 teaspoon salt
1/2 teaspoon pepper blend (see page 131)

Preheat the oven to 400 degrees F.

Combine all the ingredients thoroughly in a large mixing bowl. Roll into walnut-size balls.

Arrange these on a greased cookie sheet. Bake for 15 minutes.

Serve hot or cold.

Yield: about 15 crab balls

Hot Cheese and
Crab Appetizer

This is a finger-licking appetizer, and it is so easy a child can do it. Best of all, it can be prepared the day before, leaving you with a free hand on the day you need one.

4 ounces cheddar or jalapeño cheddar cheese spread
2 1/3 tablespoons butter
2/3 cup sifted flour
1 cup (1/2 pound) crab meat
Sliced bread; white, rye, wheat, or a mixture

Allow the cheese spread and butter to soften at room temperature. Mash all the ingredients except the bread together into a thoroughly blended paste. Divide the paste into three equal portions.

Roll each portion into a 1 inch cylinder. Wrap these cylinders in plastic wrap. Refrigerate overnight.

The following day, preheat the oven to 325 degrees F. Cut each of the cylinders into 1/2-inch-thick disks. Cut the slices of bread into quarters, enough quarters to equal the number of cheese-crab disks cut from the cylinders. The bread can be lightly buttered or brushed with garlic butter if desired.

Place 1 cheese-crab disk on each of the quarter slices of bread. Arrange these on a cookie sheet.

Bake for 25 minutes. Serve hot.

Yield: 3 to 4 dozen appetizers

Crab Meat Stuffed Jalapeños

This is a southwestern hors d'oeuvre deluxe. The recipe was developed by Annette Reddell Hegen of the Marine Advisory Service at Port Aransas, Texas. These little fellows are hot. When I serve them, I set out a generous pitcher of something cold.

Crab Meat Stuffing

2 cups (1 pound) crab meat
2 tablespoons finely chopped green bell pepper
2 tablespoons finely chopped onions
2 tablespoons finely chopped dill pickle
1/4 cup cracker meal
1 egg, beaten
1/4 teaspoon salt
1/4 teaspoon black pepper
1/8 teaspoon cayenne
1 clove minced garlic
1/4 cup milk

Breading Mix

2 cups cracker meal
1 cup milk
2 eggs, beaten
1/4 teaspoon salt
1/4 teaspoon black pepper

1 can (1 pound, 11-ounce size) whole jalapeño
   peppers
Oil for deep-frying

To make the crab meat stuffing, combine the stuffing ingredients and mix thoroughly. Set aside.

To prepare the breading mix, place the cracker meal in a flat pan or dish. In another shallow bowl, mix the milk, eggs, salt, and pepper.

To prepare the stuffed jalapeños, cut each pepper in half lengthwise. Remove the pulp and seeds, and discard them. Rinse the peppers under running water. Stuff each pepper with the crab stuffing. Press additional stuffing around the pepper.

To bread the peppers for frying, dip each pepper first in the egg mixture, then in the cracker meal. Repeat the procedure for each stuffed pepper.

Deep-fry the stuffed peppers in hot grease until golden brown. These will cook very, very quickly. Drain on absorbent paper and serve.

Yield: about 30 hors d'oeuvres

Shari Clark's Crab Egg Rolls

Shari Clark loves both crab meat and oriental food. She developed this recipe so she could have just another way to eat the two together. I like egg rolls because they are just plain fun to make. And as you can see, when you make your own egg rolls with this recipe, you don't get the heavy dose of salt that all too often comes with the restaurant variety.

1 tablespoon butter
2 Brussels sprouts finely chopped
1 cup (1/2 pound) crab meat
1/2 cup chopped celery
1/2 cup chopped green onions
1 tablespoon lemon juice
1/4 cup diced water chestnuts
2 teaspoons soy sauce

12 egg roll wrappers
1 egg, lightly beaten
Canola or peanut oil for deep-frying

To make the filling for the egg rolls, melt the butter over low heat in a heavy skillet. Add the Brussels sprouts and saute, stirring frequently, for 3 minutes. Add the remaining ingredients, stir to combine, and remove from heat.

In a separate skillet or deep pot, heat the canola or peanut oil medium to low-high for deep-frying.

To make an egg roll, lay each wrapper flat. Position the wrapper with one corner pointed toward you and another pointed away, so that the square wrapper is turned to a diamond shape. Brush the wrapper lightly with the beaten egg, as a sealer. Spoon 3 tablespoons of the crab meat mixture on the wrapper. Fold the bottom of the wrapper over the crab meat mixture, then fold in the sides. Roll the wrapper from the bottom into a tight roll. Repeat this for each egg roll.

Deep-fry each egg roll until golden brown, about 1 minute. Fry a few at a time, no more than 4 each time. Drain on absorbent paper and serve hot.

Yield: 6 servings of 2 egg rolls each

Crab Egg Roll

This is an egg roll with an interesting variety of ingredients. Egg rolls, unlike many oriental dishes familiar to people in the West, actually did originate in China. They were served with tea to guests on the Chinese New Year. In China, since the new year came in the spring, what we know as egg rolls were called spring rolls. Later, egg was added to the dough for the wrapper (some say this practice started in Canton) and the new food was called an egg roll. Whatever they are called, egg rolls are delicious. Serve them with soy sauce, hot mustard, or sweet and sour sauce on the side.

3 tablespoons peanut oil
1 cup shredded cabbage
1/4 pound fresh bean sprouts
1/2 pound fresh green beans, cut in thin, diagonal
   slices
1/2 cup shredded carrots
1/4 cup chopped onion
1 clove minced garlic
1 1/2 cup (3/4 pound) crab meat
1/4 teaspoon salt
1/4 teaspoon dry mustard

10 egg roll wrappers
1 egg, lightly beaten
Canola or peanut oil for deep-frying

Heat 3 tablespoons of peanut oil in a heavy skillet. Add the shredded cabbage. Saute, stirring constantly. Continue to saute, adding each successive ingredient from the list at 1 to 2 minute intervals up to the crab meat. Add the crab meat, salt, and mustard at the same time. Saute 2 minutes, stirring constantly to blend. Remove from the heat.

In a separate skillet, wok, or deep pot, heat the canola or peanut oil medium to low-high for deep frying.

Lay each wrapper flat. Position the wrapper with one corner pointed toward you and another pointed away, so that the square wrapper is turned to a diamond shape. Brush the wrapper lightly with the beaten egg as a sealer. Spoon 1/4 to 1/3 cup of the crab meat mixture on the wrapper. Fold the bottom of the wrapper over the crab meat mixture, then fold in the sides. Roll the wrapper from the bottom into a tight roll. Repeat this for each egg roll.

Deep-fry each egg roll until golden brown, about 1 minute. Fry no more than 4 each egg rolls each time. Drain on absorbent paper.

Serve hot.

Yield: 5 servings of 2 egg rolls each

Soups and Chowders

Crab Soup

This recipe was given to me by Clark Hollins, the scion of one of Virginia's old families. He said that this recipe has been handed down in his family for generations although he admits adding the mushrooms and spicing it up with Tabasco. One of the secrets to this soup's flavor is the long, slow cooking time. If you can wait, reduce the heat a bit and simmer still longer. The results will be even better.

2 tablespoons butter
2 tablespoons flour
1/2 cup finely chopped red onion
1 stalk celery, finely chopped including leaves
1 tablespoon chopped fresh parsley
1/4 teaspoon salt
1/4 teaspoon pepper blend (see page 131)
4 large mushrooms, finely chopped
2 cups chicken stock
1 cup milk
1 1/2 cups (3/4 pound) lump crab meat
1/8 teaspoon Tabasco
4 teaspoons sherry

Slowly melt the butter in a large, heavy skillet. Slowly add the flour, stirring constantly, until thoroughly combined into a smooth paste. Cook 3 minutes, stirring constantly.

Increase the heat slightly and add the onions, celery, parsley, salt, pepper blend, and mushrooms. Saute the mixture for an additional 5 minutes. Whisk in the chicken stock. Bring the mixture to a boil, stirring frequently. Reduce heat to very low, cover and simmer for 90 minutes. Remove the soup from the heat. Strain the liquid, forcing the vegetable pulp through a sieve. Return to the heat.

Stir in the milk, crab meat, and Tabasco sauce. Leave on the heat, stirring constantly, until the soup is thoroughly heated.

Warm the soup bowls and spoon 1 teaspoon of sherry into each. Ladle the soup into the bowls. Serve hot.

Yield: 4 servings

Cream of Crab Soup

You don't need to be overcome by a fit of ambition to make this mild, delicately flavored soup. It is simple as can be and a sure-fire winner. Sometimes for extra color and a bit of crunch I sprinkle the top with a few slivers of shredded, raw carrot or tiny green pepper cubes.

2 quarts milk
1/2 small red onion, finely chopped
2 tablespoons finely chopped celery
2 tablespoon butter
1 tablespoon flour
1 teaspoon chopped fresh parsley
1/4 teaspoon salt
1/3 teaspoon white pepper
2 cups (1 pound) lump crab meat
Paprika

Prepare a large double boiler. Combine the milk, onion, celery, butter, flour, parsley, salt, and pepper.

Cook the mixture in the double boiler 45 minutes, stirring occasionally. Add the crab meat and cook, stirring frequently, until the mixture is thoroughly heated.

Dust with paprika, and serve immediately.

Yield: 4 servings

She-Crab Soup

No book of crab recipes would be complete without that American classic from South Carolina, she-crab soup. For generations chefs in Charleston have been making their reputations with this dish.

The she-crab is a female crab carrying eggs, or roe. She-crab soup blends the eggs and the meat of the crab. Most of the older recipes used Madeira, a throwback to the days when Charleston had a direct trade with Europe. As trade took new directions, dry sherry increasingly became a substitute for Madeira.

The most finely flavored she-crab soup is made from fresh crab roe. If fresh is not available, several good brands of canned roe are on the market, but you may have to search specialty stores for a source. If you see South Carolina on the label, it is a good sign; the state has several established packers who compete for quality.

Purists will almost surely gag on the thought— I don't use crab roe. In my interest in conservation, I substitute 3 hard-boiled egg yolks, finely crumbled, for crab eggs. Unfortunately, my soup has a different flavor and is certainly not true she-crab soup. The recipe below is authentic.

2 tablespoons canola oil
1 green onion, including top, finely chopped
1 stalk celery, including leaves, finely chopped
2 tablespoons flour
3 cups milk
2 cups heavy cream
1 tablespoons chopped fresh parsley
1/4 teaspoon salt
1/3 teaspoon white pepper
2 teaspoons worcestershire
1/4 teaspoon Tabasco
3 tablespoons dry Madeira
3 cups (1 1/2 pounds) lump crab meat

Roe (eggs) from 10-15 crabs
1 hard-boiled egg, finely chopped
1/2 teaspoon paprika for dusting

Heat the canola oil in a large, heavy skillet. Add the onions and celery and cook until soft for about 3 minutes.

Add the flour a little at a time, stirring constantly. Cook for 4 minutes on moderate heat. Reduce the heat and add the milk, cream, parsley, and seasonings. Bring the mixture to a boil, stirring constantly. Cook and stir after the mixture begins to bubble for about 3 minutes.

Remove the soup from the heat. Stir in the crabmeat, roe, and egg.

Return to the heat and add the Madeira. Simmer 5 minutes. Ladle into bowls and serve hot, dusted with paprika.

Yield: 6 servings

Soft-Shell Crab Soup

Thick, hearty soups are my favorites. This soup features my two favorite seafoods, crab and shrimp, plus pasta. While many soups serve equally well as a main dishes or first courses, this is so rich that I reserve it for a main course. Once you serve it, you will want plenty anyway. On the side, serve rye, black bread, or any full-flavored breads broken into chunks and heated.

1/4 cup olive oil
4 shallots, chopped
1 garlic clove
3 large tomatoes, finely chopped
1 cup dry white wine
1 cup hot water
2 teaspoons fresh chopped parsley
1 teaspoon dried thyme
1/2 teaspoon salt
1/3 teaspoon pepper blend (see page 131)
1/8 teaspoon cayenne
1/8 teaspoon Tabasco
4 soft-shell crabs, cleaned
1 pound shrimp, shelled and deveined
1/4 pound fettuccine, broken into finger-length
    pieces

Heat the olive oil in a large heavy pot. Add the shallots, garlic, and tomatoes, and cook on medium for 4 minutes, stirring frequently. Slowly add the white wine and water. Stir in the parsley, thyme, salt, pepper blend, cayenne, and Tabasco. Bring to simmering boil. Add the cleaned crabs, cover, and cook for 25 minutes, stirring frequently.

In a separate pot, cook the fettuccine according to the directions on the package. When cooked, drain and set aside.

Remove the cooked crabs from the pot and chop into bite-size pieces. Return the chopped crabs to the pot.

Add the cleaned, deveined shrimp, and stir to combine. Continue to cook for 3 minutes.

Add the cooked fettuccine to the pot. Stir and heat until the soup is thoroughly combined and heated. Serve hot.

Yield: 4 servings

Oriental Crab Soup

Actually, this recipe did not come from the Orient. It was given to me by Kara Shelton, a friend in Los Angeles, who developed it. She wanted a soup that was easy, used common ingredients, and had an oriental flavor. The first step, cooking the mushrooms with the soy sauce, is important; the soup will loose much of its flavor if you skip the soy sauce or use canned mushrooms.

Another secret to give this soup extra zip is to make your own chicken stock. If making your own stock is not practical, search in the better stores for freshly made stock. Some stores carry it at the meat and fish counter or can direct you to where it is sold. At the very least, comparison shop to find the most flavorful canned brand in your area. Rotate your purchases of chicken stock until you have tried all the brands available to you, then select the best. The best flavor may cost a few pennies more but resist the temptation to economize in this crucial area. For an ingredient as important as this, the extra money is well spent.

2 tablespoons peanut or canola oil
1/4 cup thinly sliced mushrooms
2 tablespoons soy sauce
2 tomatoes, finely chopped
2 cups (1 pound) crab meat
2 teaspoons grated fresh ginger
4 cups chicken stock
1 tablespoon cider vinegar
2 tablespoons dry sherry
1 green onion, finely chopped, top included
2 tablespoons finely grated carrots

Heat 1 tablespoon of the oil in a heavy pot over medium low heat. Add the mushrooms and saute 1 minute, stirring constantly. Add 1 tablespoon of the soy sauce, then cook for another minute, continuing to stir constantly. Add the tomatoes, crab meat, and ginger. Cook for 4 minutes, continually turning the mixture.

Add the chicken stock, reduce the heat to low, and cook for 15 minutes, stirring frequently. Stir in the remaining ingredients. Simmer for an additional 10 minutes. Serve hot.

Yield: 4 servings

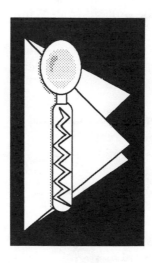

Shari Clark's Crab Dumpling Soup

The best way to make dumplings for this soup is with a ravioli maker—it crimps, cuts, and seals the dumplings in one pass. Dumplings made with a ravioli maker turn out neat and well shaped. In addition, crimping helps hold the dumpling together while cooking. Ravioli makers are simple and inexpensive. If your local cookware store does not carry them, they can be ordered from Williams-Sonoma.

When you make this recipe, there will be some waste trimmed from the egg roll wrappers. Deep-fat fry the excess, and dust with powdered sugar for an extra snack or dessert.

1 Brussels sprout, finely chopped
1/2 cup (1/4 pound) crab meat
1/4 cup finely chopped celery
1 teaspoon lemon juice
1/8 cup diced water chestnuts
2 tablespoons soy sauce

6 egg roll wrappers
1 small egg, lightly beaten
1 quart chicken broth
1/4 cup finely chopped green onion

To prepare the filling mix, finely chop the Brussels sprout. In a small, heavy pan, melt 1/2 tablespoon of butter over low heat. Saute the Brussels sprout in the butter, stirring frequently, until it is tender, about 4 minutes. Transfer to a mixing bowl. Add the remaining filling ingredients to the mixing bowl and stir until thoroughly combined. Set aside.

Brush the top of each wrapper with the lightly beaten egg. One wrapper will be the bottom of the dumplings and another will be the top.

To assemble the dumplings, place 1 teaspoon of filling about 1/2 inch from the corner of each bottom wrapper and place another teaspoon of filling in the center. Each bottom wrapper should have 5 teaspoons of filling mix spaced equally across the wrapper.

Place the top wrappers over the bottom wrappers with the filling mix. Gently press around each mound of filling to seal finger-tight. Using a ravioli maker, cut out each dumpling. (If you do not have a ravioli maker, press around each mound with a small glass to seal, then use a sharp knife to cut out each dumpling. Allow 1/4 inch margin around each dumpling.) Set the prepared dumplings aside.

In a large pot, heat the chicken stock to boiling. Drop all the dumplings into the broth. Boil 5 minutes. Serve immediately, garnished with chopped green onion.

Yield: 5 servings as a first course, or 2 as a main course

Crab Meat with Bitter Orange Soup

Bitter oranges are a traditional ingredient in Spanish dishes. They were first introduced to Europe by the Moslems who had a long history of cultivating bitter orange groves in Morocco. Today, bitter oranges are so plentiful on the Iberian peninsula that in many areas they grow wild. The Spanish name for this fruit is bigarades.

Unfortunately, bitter oranges are not yet plentiful in the United States and you may have to call specialty stores to find them. Large Hispanic markets may stock them. Bitter oranges are not the same as the sweet oranges commonly seen. Occasionally, bitter oranges are marketed as Seville oranges or as Italian blood oranges.

4 cups water
2 tablespoons olive oil
2 cloves garlic, sliced
1/3 cup thinly sliced onion
1 cup (1/2 pound) crab meat
3/4 cup bitter orange juice
1 teaspoon lemon juice

In a heavy pot, bring the water to a rolling boil. Reduce heat to simmer.

In a separate pan, heat the oil. Add the garlic and saute 5 minutes on low heat. Remove the garlic and discard. Add the onion and saute 7 minutes.

Transfer the onion to the simmering water. Cook 20 minutes, then stir in the crab meat. Simmer an additional 2 minutes, then add the bitter orange and lemon juices.

Serve immediately. This soup can be refrigerated and reheated.

Yield: 4 servings

Crab Chowder

This is a rich, finely flavored chowder that is as easy to prepare as it is good to eat. The potatoes give the chowder extra body. I think that it is an expecially good on cold winter days. I serve it with garlic croutons sprinkled over the top. The word chowder is derived from *chaudière*, the French word for the large, heavy iron pot that once dominated French country kitchens.

6 tablespoons butter
1/2 cup finely chopped red onion
1/3 cup finely chopped green onion
1 medium tomato, chopped
1/3 cup finely chopped celery
1 cup water
3 medium baking potatoes, peeled and diced
2 cups milk
2 cups (1 pound) lump crab meat
1/4 teaspoon Tabasco
1/2 teaspoon pepper blend (see page 131)
1/4 teaspoon salt

Using a large, heavy pot, melt the butter over low heat. Add the red onion, green onions, tomato, and celery. Cook over low heat for 7 minutes. Add the water to the mixture in a slow stream. Increase the heat and bring the water to boiling. Add the potatoes, reduce the heat to simmer, and cook 50 minutes.

Stir in the crab meat and the remaining ingredients. Cook, stirring frequently, until the soup returns to simmering boil. Serve immediately.

Yield: 4 servings

Crab Cioppino

Crab cioppino can be the center of a very informal or formal meal, as suitable for a terrace or patio as a dining room. Cioppino began along the wharves of San Francisco as a means of using odds and ends from the fishermen's catches. The dish soon earned a reputation as a meal to write home about. It seems that everyone in San Francisco has a favorite recipe, all different and all delicious. I like to serve cioppino with heaps of buttered garlic bread to people who aren't quite sure if a meal is a party or if a party is a meal.

You can make good crab cioppino with this recipe using almost any sort of crab meat, but it will not be authentic cioppino unless you use Dungeness crab, the largest and most sought-after crab on the U.S. Pacific coast.

4 large Dungeness crabs, cleaned (4 cups, or 2 pounds of crab meat)

1 clove garlic, minced
1 cup chopped onion
1/2 cup water
1/4 cup dry white wine
1 cup olive oil
2 No. 2 cans tomatoes
2 tablespoons tomato paste
1/4 cup chopped fresh basil
2 tablespoons chopped fresh rosemary
1/4 teaspoon salt
1/2 teaspoon pepper blend (see page 131)

To prepare the cleaned Dungeness crab, break off the claws first. Using a mallet or nutcracker, crack open the claws. Set aside with the crab.

Place the cleaned crabs and the cracked claws in a large pot. Add the garlic, onion, water, wine, and olive oil. Cover and simmer for 20 minutes.

In a separate pan, heat the tomato paste along with the tomatoes and half of their juice. When the mixture is thoroughly heated, add it to the pot containing the crabs.

Add the basil, rosemary, salt, and pepper blend. Continue to simmer for an additional half hour. Serve hot.

Yield: 8 servings

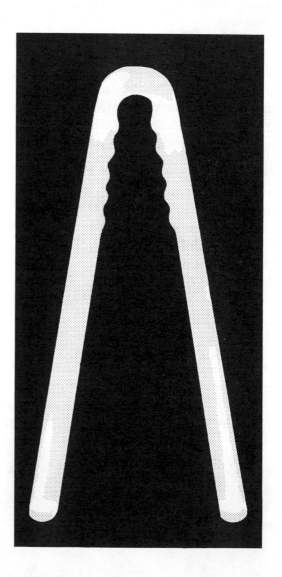

Crab Gumbo

Gumbo borrows a little something from everywhere, even its name. Gumbo came with Africans on slave ships from the Congo. The African name for okra was *quingombo*. Since okra is a staple ingredient in this dish, quingombo was soon shortened to gumbo.

The making of gumbo has always been an invitation to experiment, and the best gumbo cooks are the most creative. Thickening is important in making fine gumbo. This recipe uses okra as a thickening agent. Many gumbos are thickened with file powder. File is the ground leaves of the sassafras tree. It can be found in the spice section of most large grocery stores. If this gumbo recipe is not thick enough for your taste, stir in a bit of ground file after the gumbo has finished cooking.

4 tablespoons bacon grease
6 tablespoons flour
1/2 clove garlic
1 green bell pepper
2 green onions, tops included
2 medium onions
2 stalks celery, leaves included
2 pounds okra
1 bay leaf, crumbled
1 No. 2 can tomatoes, juice included
2 small cans tomato paste
6 cups chicken stock
4 cups (2 pounds) crab meat
1 pound shrimp, shelled and deveined
1 teaspoon salt
2 teaspoons pepper blend (see page 131)
1/2 teaspoon cayenne
1/2 teaspoon Tabasco
6 cups cooked rice

Using a large, heavy pot, melt the bacon grease over low heat. Add the flour slowly, stirring constantly to make a smooth roux.

Finely chop the garlic. Chop the green pepper, onions, celery, and okra. Crumble the bay leaf. Add to the roux, then stir to combine. Increase the heat slightly and cook 20 minutes, stirring frequently.

Add the tomatoes, including their juice, and the tomato paste. Stir to combine. Pour in the chicken stock. Reduce the heat and simmer the mixture for 1 1/4 hours, stirring occasionally.

Add the crab meat, stir until the mixture is thoroughly combined, and simmer 10 minutes. Add the shrimp, stir the mixture, and simmer an additional 5 minutes. Stir in the salt, pepper blend, cayenne, and Tabasco. Serve immediately with cooked rice.

Yield: 8 servings

Gazpacho with Crab Meat

This gazpacho may seem to have a long list of ingredients, but it is worth the effort. Actually, the soup is very easy to make. Almost everything goes in the pot at once. The hardest thing is waiting for the ingredients to simmer and release their flavors before you plunge your ladle in for a taste!

This gazpacho is an appetizer fit for starting your most elegant evenings. It is also a dynamite meal standing on its own. I like to serve it with a small green salad and French toast with a thin layer of melted Parmesan cheese.

2 1/2 cups tomato juice
1 cup (1/2 pound) lump crab meat
3 tablespoons red wine vinegar
1/4 cup peanut or canola oil
2 pounds tomatoes, peeled, cored, and finely chopped
1 medium cucumber, chopped
1/2 cup finely chopped green bell pepper
1/2 cup finely chopped red onion
1/2 teaspoon salt
1 teaspoon Pickapeppa Sauce
1/4 teaspoon garlic powder
1/2 teaspoon pepper blend (see page 131)
1/4 teaspoon Tabasco
3 tablespoons salsa (optional)

In a heavy pot, heat the tomato juice over medium heat until it just begins to boil. Add the remaining ingredients, except the Tabasco and salsa.

Stir the mixture, reduce the heat to simmer, and cook for 45 minutes, stirring frequently.

Add the Tabasco and salsa. Stir until thoroughly combined and heat thoroughly. Remove from the heat. Refrigerate until thoroughly chilled. Serve cold.

Yield: 4 servings

Cooking in the Shell— Whole Crabs, Claws and Legs, Soft-Shell Crabs

Boiled Blue Crabs

This is the most basic recipe for cooking blue crabs. Since crab meat in this book means cooked crab meat, you will need to know this if you catch or buy live crabs. Boiled blue crabs served with lemon butter, lime butter, French bread, and white wine are just great. They are always good served plain, too.

24 blue crabs
6 quarts water
1/3 cup salt

Wash the crabs thoroughly under fresh running water. Be sure that they are all alive and active. Set the crabs aside.

Pour the water in a large covered pot and bring to a rapid boil. Add the salt and drop the crabs into the water. Cover the pot and reduce the heat.

Simmer the crabs for 15 minutes, or until the crabs turn bright red. Remove the crabs from the boiling water and serve immediately. Set the table with nutcrackers, picks, extra plates, and plenty of napkins.

Yield: 6 servings

Steamed Blue Crabs

Cooking crabs by steaming offers an advantage to vegetable lovers. While steaming crabs, it is easy to rig a second steaming rack above the crabs and fill this with corn, carrots, onions, and other good things. Also, steam cooks with less water, an important advantage if you are cooking outdoors and have to carry your fixings to the cooking site.

3 cups water
3 tablespoons salt
16 blue crabs
1 stick butter
1/2 lemon

Prepare a steaming rack in the bottom of a large pot. The rack must be placed so that the crabs will not touch the boiling liquid. Cover the bottom of the pot with 1 inch of water.

Bring the water to a vigorous boil.

Add the salt, then add the crabs in layers.

Reduce heat and steam until crabs turn bright red, about 15 minutes.

While the crabs are steaming, slowly melt the butter in a separate pan. After the butter has melted, squeeze in the lemon juice.

Serve the crabs immediately after steaming, serving the lemon butter as a dipping sauce. Be sure to bring nut crackers, picks, extra plates (for the discarded shells), and plenty of napkins to the table.

Yield: 4 servings

Boiled Dungeness Crabs

Blue crabs take their name from their bright blue color, but the way Dungeness acquired their name is less obvious. Dalton Hobbs with the Oregon State Seafood Marketing Program helped me get this information.

In the eighteenth century the English explorer George Vancouver charted what later became the U.S. northern Pacific coast. When Captain Vancouver sailed into the Strait of Juan de Fuca he named one point New Dungeness, "From its great resemblance to Dungeness in the British Channel." British subjects later settled the Strait of Juan de Fuca and found the waters teeming with a crab that reminded them of the [European] common crab caught near their former homes. They eagerly captured it for food.

The settlers called this crab the Dungeness crab after the area in the New World where it was first discovered. As English settlement moved south, the name given by the people of the Northwest Territories traveled wherever the Dungeness crab was fished. Today, it is known to crab lovers throughout the United States.

There are two ways to boil this tasty denizen of the Pacific Northwest, either before or after cleaning. No matter which method you choose, there will be someone ready to swear that the other way is the only correct one. In this argument, I think that both camps are wrong; I think that Dungeness is excellent cooked both ways. Feel free to experiment and find the way that you prefer.

To boil Dungeness crabs before cleaning, you have merely to keep the crabs alive and active until they go in the pot. Rinse the crabs in running water, then drop each crab into the pot head first. Cover and continue boiling until the crabs turn bright red, 10 to 13 minutes.

Remove the crabs from the boiling water and serve immediately with nutcrackers, mallets, picks, extra plates, and plenty of napkins.

To boil Dungeness crabs after cleaning, you must either kill and clean the crabs yourself or ask your fishmonger to do it for you. It is certainly easier than doing it yourself. After the crab has been killed and dressed, be prepared to cook it straightaway; the crab will quickly spoil if left uncooked.

Instructions for killing and cleaning a Dungeness crab are included on page 100. They will tell you how to clean the crab quickly and easily.

To cook the cleaned crab, rinse it under running water. Don't forget to rinse the body cavity. Place the crabs in boiling water, cover, and simmer until the crabs turn bright red, about 15 minutes. Since the body cavity of a cleaned crab is open to the boiling water, a cleaned Dungeness does not require a rolling boil for cooking. When the crabs are cooked, remove them from the pot, drain, pat dry, and serve immediately with the same cracking tools detailed above.

Yield: 3 crabs = 6 servings

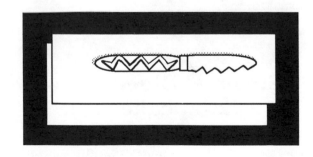

Crabs Steamed in Beer

Start this recipe with your favorite crab boil. Use the crab boil recipe given on page 130, devise your own, or buy one of the commercial preparations. Zatarain's Crab Boil and Old Bay Seasoning are good brands, well tested by generations of cooks.

16 blue crabs
1/4 cup crab boil
2 tablespoons salt
2 cans beer
1 1/2 cups cider vinegar

Prepare a steaming rack in the bottom of a large pot. The rack must be placed so that the crabs will not touch the boiling liquid. Put the crabs on the steaming rack.

Combine the seasonings, beer, and vinegar in a bowl. Stir until thoroughly mixed, then pour over the crabs into the pot. Bring the liquid to a vigorous boil over high heat. Reduce heat and steam until crabs turn bright red, about 15 minutes.

Yield: 4 servings

Steamed Blue Crabs— Chesapeake Style

Many seasoning mixes may be readily substituted for commercial crab boils. I think that the blend of flavors used here is particularly appealing. This recipe was given to me by Jack Watson, a native of the Chesapeake Bay area who has cooked and eaten crabs in just about every way imaginable. He says that this is his best recipe for steaming.

3 cups beer
2 cups white vinegar
2 tablespoons salt
1 tablespoon black pepper
1 tablespoon dry mustard
1 teaspoon cayenne
1 teaspoon curry powder

24 blue crabs

1 stick butter
1/2 lemon

Combine the beer, vinegar, and seasonings. Stir until thoroughly blended.

Prepare a steaming rack in the bottom of a large pot. The rack must be placed so that the crabs will not touch the boiling liquid.

Place half of the crabs in the pot on the steaming rack. Pour half of the beer-seasoning mix over the crabs. Add the remaining crabs. Pour the remaining beer-seasoning mix over the crabs.

Bring the liquid to a boil and steam until the crabs turn bright red, about 20 minutes.

While the crabs are steaming, slowly melt the butter in a separate pan and squeeze in the lemon juice.

Serve the crabs immediately after steaming, serving the lemon butter as a dipping sauce. Be sure to bring nut crackers, picks, extra plates for the discarded shells, and plenty of napkins to the table.

Yield: 6 servings

Barbecued Blue Crabs with Orange Sauce

Everything tastes terrific off the open grill. Cooking out is so quick, easy, and delicious I never tire of it. And when the citrus tang of orange and lime is thrown in with the sweet flavor of honey, a sure fire hit is in the making!

To get extra flavor from the crabs, examine the crabs for fat deposits. Crab fats are rich in taste. When you clean the crabs, leave any fat deposits you find in the crab for cooking. If you have some crabs that are fat and others that are lean, try one of each to savor the difference. Grilled corn-on-the-cob and other vegetables are good with this.

16 blue crabs
1 gallon water
1/4 cup salt

Orange Sauce

1/2 cup fresh orange juice
1/2 cup ketchup
2 tablespoons lime juice
1 tablespoon soy sauce
1/8 teaspoon onion powder
1/8 teaspoon garlic powder
2 tablespoons honey
1 tablespoon brown sugar

If the crabs have not been boiled, prepare them by washing them thoroughly under fresh running water. Be sure that they are all alive and active. Set the crabs aside.

Pour 1 gallon of water in a large covered pot. Bring the water to a rapid boil, then add 1/4 cup salt. Drop the crabs into the water. Cover the pot and reduce the heat. Simmer the crabs for 15 minutes, or until they turn bright red. Remove the crabs from the boiling water, drain, and set aside.

To prepare the Orange Sauce, combine all the remaining ingredients except the brown sugar and honey. Heat over low heat, then pour in the honey and stir in the brown sugar and stir. Continue to cook for an additional 4 minutes over low heat, stirring frequently. Remove and keep warm.

Crack the claws of the boiled crabs, but leave the shell over the claw meat. Remove the legs and top shell of each crab. Clean the body cavity of the crab. Instructions for cleaning a boiled blue crab are on page 7.

Place the cleaned crabs on the grill about 12 inches above the heat source. Place the crabs on the grill with the shell down, facing the heat source.

Brush the crabs liberally with Orange Sauce. Grill 20 to 30 minutes. Baste the body cavity of the crabs 2 or 3 times while cooking.

Serve hot, along with nutcrackers, picks, extra plates, and plenty of napkins. Serve extra sauce for dipping.

Yield: 4 servings; 1 cup sauce

Broiled Dungeness Crab

This broiler recipe also works on the outdoor grill, but you need to adjust the time carefully. High heat tends to dry out crab meat rapidly. Save the juicy sweetness and flavor of the crabs while broiling by frequent basting.

2 Dungeness crabs, cleaned

1/2 cup butter, divided
1 clove garlic
1 sliced ring from a large white onion
1/2 cup white wine
1 lemon, cut in half
1 lemon, sliced for garnish

To prepare the cleaned crabs for broiling, remove the top shell. Cut the crabs in half. Crack the claws. Set aside.

Preheat the broiler.

To prepare the basting sauce, melt 2 tablespoons of the butter in a heavy skillet over low heat. Slice the garlic clove in half. Saute the garlic halves and the onion ring in the butter until both are tender and golden, about 4 minutes. Remove the garlic and onion and discard.

Add the remaining butter to the skillet and heat until melted. After the butter has melted, slowly stir in the white wine.

To broil the Dungeness crabs, arrange the crab halves bottom side down in a broiling pan. Baste liberally with the basting sauce. Cook the crabs, about 5 minutes on each side, basting frequently. It is only necessary to turn the crabs once.

Sprinkle the crabs with lemon juice immediately after removing from the heat. Serve at once with lemon slices.

Yield: 4 servings

Fried Stone Crab Claws

Stone crab claws are one of the world's premier foods. They truly deserve the most careful preparation you can give them. When frying stone crab claws, I use clarified butter and the finest cooking oil available. It is a bit more trouble, but the result is worth it.

6 stone crab claws, steamed
1 egg
1/2 cup self-rising flour
1 teaspoon salt
1 teaspoon black pepper
Clarified butter

If the crab claws have not been steamed, prepare them by placing a steaming rack in the bottom of a large pot. The rack must be placed so that the crabs will not touch the boiling liquid. Add about 3/4 inch of water to the bottom of the pot and bring to a rapid boil. Steam the claws until they turn a brilliant coral, about 10 minutes. The splash of black color on the tip of the claw will not turn red.

To prepare fried crab claws, crack the steamed crab claws with a hammer or heavy nutcracker. Take care when cracking not to press so hard that you drive pieces of the broken shell into the tender meat below. Carefully pick out the meat, keeping the pieces in large chunks.

Combine the flour, salt, and pepper. Set aside. Lightly beat the egg. Set aside.

Dip each crab claw in egg, let the excess drain off, then roll it lightly in the flour mixture. Repeat this procedure a second time.

Over medium heat, fry the claws in clarified butter until golden brown, turning each claw once. Do not overcook; the meat has already been steamed. Serve immediately.

Yield: 2 servings

Steamed Stone Crab Claws with Lemon Butter or Mustard Sauce

The meat of the stone crab's claw is so sweet you should not smother its delicate flavor in a heavy or strongly flavored sauce. I use sauce to complement, not overpower, the flavor. My favorite accompaniment for stone crab claws is lemon butter, also a favorite in southern Florida, home of the people who know stone crabs best. Another popular southern Florida stone crab sauce is mustard sauce.

12 stone crab claws

Lemon Butter
1 stick unsalted butter
1 large lemon, cut in half
1 lemon, cut in wedges, as garnish

Mustard Sauce
1/2 cup sour cream
1 1/2 tablespoons prepared mustard
2 teaspoons melted butter
1/2 teaspoon fresh chopped parsley
1/8 teaspoon salt

To steam the crab claws, place the claws on a rack in a covered pot or steamer containing an inch or so of boiling water. Make sure that the boiling water does not touch the rack. Steam until the claws turn to brilliant coral. Remove from heat immediately.

Stone crab claws can be tough to crack. If a nutcracker can do the job, so much the better. You may, however, need to use a hammer or mallet. Take care that, in breaking the hard shell, you do not drive the pieces of bone into the tender meat.

To prepare lemon butter, melt a stick of butter slowly over low heat. Do not allow to brown. Give the butter a good squeeze of lemon before taking it to the table. Serve warm with additional lemon wedges on the side. Lime works the same way as lemon in this recipe, and many prefer it.

To prepare mustard sauce, combine the ingredients. Heat on low until just warm, stirring occasionally. Serve warm.

Yield: 4 servings

Broiled King Crab Legs

This recipe was developed for the broiler but will also work on the outdoor grill. If you use a charcoal grill, you should cook with the slit side of the crab leg up.

As always when grilling or broiling, you simply cannot baste the crabs too often. Crab meat dries rapidly when exposed to direct heat. Baste before cooking and as often as practical while cooking. Your reward will be tender, flavorful meat.

Unless you are cooking in Alaska where king crabs are caught, your crab legs were cooked before shipping. You need cook them only long enough to heat the meat thoroughly and impart the rich, broiled flavor you will enjoy.

1/2 cub butter
1/4 cup lemon or lime juice
1/4 cup soy sauce

8 large sections of king crab legs

To prepare the basting sauce, melt the butter over low heat. Remove from the heat and add the remaining ingredients. This is good for both a basting and a dipping sauce.

To prepare the crab legs for broiling, make a long slit on the underside of each crab leg. A sharp, thin-bladed knife is excellent for this purpose. Always cut away from you; crab legs can have rather tough skin and it is not unusual for a knife to slip. After the cut has been made, wiggle the blade back and forth to make an opening large enough to let the basting sauce get in.

Preheat the broiler. Broil the crab legs with the slit side up, basting frequently, for 3 to 5 minutes. Serve immediately with extra sauce for dipping.

Yield: 4 servings

Sauteed Soft-Shell Crabs

You will search the bookshelf in vain looking for an easier way to add elegance and zest to a dish than with this simple Butter Pecan Sauce. The sauce is particularly easy to prepare and you can substitute any nut for the pecans.

4 tablespoons milk
1/2 cup flour
1/2 teaspoon salt
1/2 teaspoon pepper blend (see page 131)
4 soft-shell crabs, cleaned

6 tablespoons butter

Butter Pecan Sauce (Optional)
1 tablespoon butter
2 tablespoons roughly chopped pecans

Place the milk in one shallow pan and the flour in another. Add the salt and pepper blend to the flour and stir with a fork. Dredge each of the cleaned crabs first in the milk and then in the flour. Shake off any excess and set aside.

Using a heavy skillet, melt the butter over low heat. Saute the crabs in the butter until done, about 5 minutes for each side. Drain on absorbent paper and keep warm.

To make butter pecan sauce, slowly melt 1 tablespoon of butter in a small saucepan. When the butter is melted, add the pecans to the pan and cook until brown, about 3 minutes. Pour the sauce over the cooked crabs immediately before serving. Serve immediately.

Yield: 2 servings

Soft-Shell Crabs—
Sauteed in Batter

This is the recipe that taught me to treat soft-shell crabs with the respect they deserve. Until I cooked this dish, I confess that I had been afraid of soft-shells. Something in me, a little voice in the back of my mind, told me that eating the whole crab was somehow wrong, not the first time that I've lied to myself. The soft-shell crabs were easy to saute and delicious. Now they have a special place on my table. I serve this with tartar sauce on the side.

2 eggs
1/4 cup milk
1 cup flour
1/2 teaspoon salt
3/4 teaspoon pepper blend (see page 131)
1 cup dried bread crumbs (about 3 slices)
12 soft-shell crabs, cleaned
Canola or peanut oil to saute

Combine the eggs and the milk in a shallow pan. Stir until blended and set aside.

In a shallow pan, mix the flour, salt, pepper blend, and bread crumbs. Stir to combine. Set aside.

Dip each cleaned soft-shell crab first in the egg batter, then in the flour. Shake off any excess.

Pour a shallow layer of oil in a heavy skillet. Heat to medium. Saute each of the soft-shell crabs in turn, about 5 minutes or until done. As each crab is done, drain on absorbent paper and keep warm. Serve hot.

Yield: 6 servings

Sauteed Soft-Shell Crabs
with Wine Sauce

I pass along with minimum comment that at odd times in history crabs have been eaten as an aphrodisiac. All I am willing to state in print is that it is easy to fall in love with this dish.

1 egg, lightly beaten
1 tablespoon milk
1/4 cup flour
1/2 teaspoon salt
1/4 teaspoon white pepper
4 soft-shell crabs, cleaned
1/4 cup butter
1/2 clove garlic, finely chopped
1 tablespoon fresh basil
1/4 cup dry white wine
1 tablespoon lime juice

In a shallow pan, lightly beat the egg. Stir in the milk and set aside.

Mix the flour, salt, and pepper in a shallow pan. Stir with a fork until thoroughly combined. Set aside.

To prepare the cleaned crabs for frying, dip each crab in the flour mixture, then the egg, and then the flour again. Shake off any excess batter.

In a heavy skillet, melt the butter over low heat. Increase the heat and saute the battered crabs until done, about 5 minutes on each side. As each crab is done, drain on absorbent and hold in a warm oven.

After cooking the crabs, use the same skillet to saute the garlic and basil. After cooking 4 minutes, add the wine and lime juice. Bring to a boil, then reduce the heat and simmer 2 minutes. Use this sauce to baste the crabs liberally before serving.

Serve hot.

Yield: 2 servings

Soft-Shell Crabs with Spiced Sherried Walnuts

Victoria Johnson from Annapolis, Maryland, gave me this recipe. She got it from her aunt who never got around to telling her the origin. I think that it is one of the best recipes I have. I like the combination of spices. Incidentally, when I call for a pinch I mean a large pinch.

3 tablespoons brown sugar
1 teaspoon white corn syrup
1 1/2 teaspoon dry sherry
1 pinch cinnamon
1 pinch allspice
1 pinch cloves
1 cup walnut halves

12 soft-shell crabs, cleaned
3/4 cup butter
1/4 teaspoon salt
1/4 teaspoon pepper blend (see page 131)

To make the spiced sherried walnuts, combine the ingredients, except the walnut halves, in a small saucepan. Heat very slowly, stirring constantly, until the sugar is melted. Add the walnut halves to the saucepan and toss to coat. Remove from the heat and spread the walnut halves on waxed paper. Set aside to cool.

Preheat the oven to 225 degrees F.

To prepare the crabs, melt the butter in a skillet in a heavy skillet over low heat. Season with the salt and pepper blend. Increase the heat to medium and fry the cleaned crabs 5 minutes on each side, or until done. Remove the crabs from the skillet and keep warm in the oven. Reserve the pan juices.

Add the spiced, sherried walnuts to the crab pan juices. Saute for 3 minutes. Pour the walnuts and pan juices over the warm crabs. Serve immediately.

Yield: 6 servings

Deep-Fried Soft-Shell Crabs

Soft-shell crabs can be fried by following the recipe in this book for Spicy, Deep-Fried Soft-Shell Crabs (see next page) or use this recipe for a more crisp, crunchy crust. Soft-shell crabs that have been frozen lose some of their springy texture, so deep-frying is especially good for previously frozen soft-shells.

1 egg, lightly beaten
2 tablespoons milk
1/2 cup flour
1/2 teaspoon salt
1/2 teaspoon pepper blend (see page 131)
1 cup dried bread crumbs (about 3 slices)
8 soft-shell crabs, cleaned
Canola or peanut oil to deep-fry

Lightly beat the egg in a shallow pan. Stir in the milk and set asiden.

Mix the flour, salt, pepper blend, and bread crumbs in a shallow pan. Stir with a fork until thoroughly combined. Set aside.

To prepare the cleaned crabs for frying, dip each crab in the flour mixture, then the egg, and then the flour again. Shake off any excess batter.

Use enough oil to cover the bottom of a deep skillet with about 2 inches of oil. Fry the crabs on medium heat until golden, about 2 to 4 minutes. Drain on absorbent paper and serve hot.

Yield: 2 servings

Spicy, Deep-Fried Soft-Shell Crabs

Willie Crussol gave me this recipe for deep-fried crabs. Willie was born and raised (most of the time, as he says) in Louisiana on the eastern shore of Lake Pontchartrain. This is serious crab country. Willie said when he was growing up near Mandeville that his family got together every weekend under the trees in the backyard and cooked crabs and whatever else they had caught. When soft-shells were in season, this was one of the recipes they used.

1 egg, lightly beaten
1 teaspoon Tabasco
1/2 cup flour
1/2 cup yellow corn meal
2 teaspoon white pepper
2 teaspoon black pepper
1/4 teaspoon cayenne
1/4 teaspoon salt
8 soft-shell crabs, cleaned
Canola or peanut oil to deep-fry

Lightly beat the egg. Stir in the Tabasco. Set aside.

Mix the flour, corn meal, and seasonings in a shallow pan. Stir with a fork until thoroughly combined. Set aside.

To prepare the cleaned crabs for frying, dip each crab in the flour mixture, then the egg, and then the flour again. Shake off any excess batter.

Use enough oil to cover the bottom of a deep skillet with about 2 inches of oil. Fry the crabs on medium heat until golden, about 2 to 4 minutes. Drain on absorbent paper and serve hot.

Yield: 4 servings

Long Island Broiled Soft-Shell Crabs

You can't get any simpler or any better than this. Recipes similar to this are common to all blue crab waters. This recipe came from the kitchen of Long Island artist Andrea Wallace. Ms. Wallace said that she wrote down just what she had seen her mother do. She suggests serving this with lemon wedges and a ramekin of melted butter.

8 soft-shell crabs, cleaned
1 stick of softened butter
1 teaspoon salt
1 teaspoon black pepper
Lemon wedges, for garnish

Preheat the broiler to moderate heat.

Rub the cleaned crabs all over with the softened butter. Melt a the rest of the stick for basting.

Arrange the crabs in a shallow broiler-proof pan or dish. Broil until they are bright red, just a few minutes. Turn the crabs once. Several times while broiling, baste with the melted butter.

Remove the crabs from the broiler and sprinkle with the salt and pepper and serve with melted butter and lemon wedges.

Yield: 4 servings

Spicy, Broiled Soft-Shell Crabs

This recipe combines the ease of the broiler with the hot, spicy flavor of the Caribbean. I re-created this dish from a meal I enjoyed once in the Bahamas. One of the secrets in preparing this dish is basting during the broiling process. Keep a brush or long-handled spoon handy so that the crabs can be kept moist while cooking. Frequent basting will also help the crabs absorb the delicious sauce.

8 soft-shell crabs, cleaned

1 tablespoon paprika
1/2 teaspoon cayenne
1 teaspoon garlic powder
1 teaspoon onion powder
1 teaspoon salt
1/2 teaspoon black pepper
1/2 cup canola or peanut oil
1/2 cup tomato sauce
1 small tomato, finely chopped
1 small tomato, coarsely chopped
1/2 teaspoon Tabasco
1/2 lime, juice of

Cut each cleaned crab into quarters. Arrange the crabs in a shallow broiler-proof dish or pan. Preheat the broiler.

Combine the spices in a small mixing bowl. Add the oil, tomato sauce, chopped tomatoes, and Tabasco. Pour the spiced sauce mix over the crab quarters. Sprinkle with the lime juice.

Broil the crabs until one side is crisply done, about 2 to 4 minutes. Turn the crabs, baste liberally, and repeat. If basting sauce runs low, use additional oil. Serve hot.

Yield: 4 servings

Broiled Soft-Shell Crabs

Whip up this luscious feast when company is in the house and watch the eager faces light up. Serve it with a simple green salad and good bread. Don't forget the lime juice, it adds a hint of aroma and a refreshing zing. This can be a bit on the hot side. You can reduce the heat by halving the amount of white pepper and eliminating the cayenne.

8 soft-shell crabs, cleaned
1 teaspoon onion powder
1 teaspoon garlic powder
2 teaspoon salt
1/4 teaspoon white pepper
1/4 teaspoon cayenne
1/4 teaspoon black pepper
2 teaspoons dried parsley
1/2 cup canola or peanut oil
1 lime, juice of

To prepare the crab for broiling, cut each cleaned crab into quarters. Arrange the crabs in a shallow broiler-proof dish or pan. Preheat the broiler.

Combine the onion powder, garlic powder, salt, white pepper, cayenne, black pepper, and parsley in a small bowl. Set aside.

Pour the oil over the crab quarters. Immediately sprinkle with the lime juice. Sprinkle the seasoning mix over the crab quarters.

Broil the crabs until one side is crisply done, about 2 to 4 minutes. Turn the crabs and repeat. When done, drain on absorbent paper and serve hot.

Yield: 4 servings

Simple Stuffed Soft-Shell Crabs

This is a first-class meal, simple as can be and fit for a king. All you need to serve with it are French bread and a good white wine. This recipe is also a good starting place to begin learning what, if anything, you would like to add to make your own stuffing for soft-shell crab.

1 stick butter
1 pound lump crab meat
2 tablespoons dry white wine (optional)
12 soft-shell crabs, cleaned

Preheat the oven to 400 degrees F.

To make the stuffing for the crabs, melt the butter in a heavy skillet over low heat. Increase the heat slightly and add the lump crab meat and the wine, if desired. If you are making this recipe without the wine, simply cook the crab meat until hot, then remove from the heat. If you are using the wine with this recipe, allow the stuffing to simmer for 2 minutes.

Arrange the cleaned crabs in a shallow baking pan. Remove the top shell from each crab and set aside. Stuff the body cavity of each of the soft-shell crabs with equal portions of the lump crab meat. Replace the top shell.

Pour the melted butter evenly over the crabs. Bake the crabs for 15 minutes, or until the crab shells turn red and the crabs have browned slightly. Serve immediately.

Yield: 6 servings

Grilled Soft-Shelled Crab Sandwiches ✓

In many parts of the United States, soft-shell crab sandwiches are almost unknown, but in the Chesapeake Bay area they are a traditional delicacy. As a substitute to the lime butter sauce, use Cajun mayonnaise or mustard sauce; either is excellent. Tartar sauce is another traditional sandwich spread for soft-shell crabs.

Marinade

1/4 cup peanut oil
1/8 teaspoon garlic powder
1/8 teaspoon cloves
1/8 teaspoon mace
1/8 teaspoon allspice
1/4 teaspoon salt
1/2 teaspoon pepper blend (see page 131)

6 soft-shell crabs, cleaned

Lime Butter

1/4 cup butter
1 tablespoon lime juice

6 English muffins, split in half and slightly flattened

To make the marinade, combine the ingredients in a shallow pan and stir until blended. Set aside.

To prepare the crabs for grilling, arrange the cleaned crabs in the marinade pan. Coat the crabs with the mixture, then turn and coat the other side. Cover, place in the refrigerator, and allow to marinate for at least 2 hours.

Prepare the grill or preheat the broiler.

Make lime butter by melting the butter on low heat in a small saucepan. Stir in the lime juice. Set aside.

Remove the marinated crabs from the marinade and place on the grill or in the broiler. Baste the crabs liberally with the marinade before and during cooking. Cook each crab until done, about 5 minutes on each side, until they are bright red.

Grill or broil the muffin halves until crisp, turning once. While grilling, brush the inside half of each muffin with the lime butter.

Assemble the sandwiches by placing each grilled soft-shell crab between 2 of the muffin halves.

Serve immediately.

Yield: 6 servings

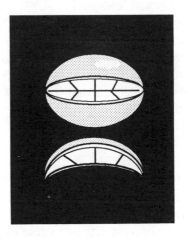

Grilled Soft-Shell Crabs with Mango-Chardonnay Sauce

This recipe comes from southern Florida. The mango-chardonnay sauce is not only elegant, it will appeal to your guests with a sweet tooth. Round this out with bananas Foster for a dynamite finale. And be prepared with pencil and paper. People always ask for this recipe.

Basting Sauce
2 tablespoons water
2 tablespoons light rum
1/2 cup soy sauce
1 tablespoon pepper blend (see page 131)
1/2 teaspoon ground cloves
1/4 cup brown sugar
2 tablespoons lime zest
1/2 stick butter

Mango-Chardonnay Sauce

3 ripe mango, peeled, cut away from pit
1 cup Chardonnay
1 tablespoon lime juice
1 large orange, juiced

8 soft-shell crabs, cleaned

Prepare the grill or preheat the broiler.
To make the basting sauce, combine the water, light rum, soy sauce, pepper blend, cloves, brown sugar, and lime zest in a small skillet or saucepan. Heat on very low heat, stirring constantly, until the brown sugar is dissolved and the ingredients are thoroughly combined. Simmer for 6 minutes, then add the butter and stir until the butter has melted.

To make the mango sauce, place the ingredients in a blender or food processor and puree. Serve at room temperature beside the grilled or broiled crabs.

To prepare the cleaned crabs for grilling or broiling, baste liberally with the basting sauce. Cook each crab until done, about 5 minutes on each side. When done, the crabs will turn bright red. Brush with the basting sauce several times during the cooking process, and immediately before serving.

Yield: 4 servings

Valentine Love Letters

If you make this for your favorite valentine, here is a little something extra to make this dish really special. Search the produce section for a red bell pepper that is slightly misshapen with a heart shaped cross section. It does not have to be exact, you can push it around some after you have sliced the pepper. Slice the pepper in about 1/2 inch thick strips. After you put the crab in the foil, arrange the heart on the crab before sealing. You can help the shape along with toothpicks if needed; you may need to rearrange it after cooking anyway. The little red heart is a nice touch.

4 soft-shell crabs, cleaned
Milk to cover crabs
3 tablespoons clarified butter
1/2 garlic clove, quartered
1 teaspoon finely chopped shallots
1 teaspoon finely chopped chives
1/8 teaspoon salt
1/8 teaspoon pepper blend (see page 131)
1/8 teaspoon paprika

Place the cleaned crabs in a pot or pan. Cover them with milk and allow to soak for 1 hour.

Preheat the broiler.

To make clarified butter, slowly melt the butter in a saucepan. Remove from the heat and allow the oil and the sediments to separate. Drain the clear, clarified butter from the top of the mixture.

To cook Valentine Love Letters, place a small amount of the butter in a heavy skillet on low heat. Add the garlic, shallots, and chives. Increase the heat and saute 2 minutes, stirring frequently. Discard the garlic.

Add the salt, pepper blend, paprika, and remaining butter. Stir. Remove from the heat as soon as the butter is fully melted.

Prepare foil envelopes large enough to contain each crab. Remove crabs from milk. Place a crab in each envelope. Pour the butter mixture over each crab. Fold the edges of the foil together to seal in the crab and the sauce.

Place on the grill directly over hottest part of coals. Broil until the crabs are bright red, about 5 to 8 minutes. Serve immediately.

Yield: 2 servings

Crab Amandine

When I put almonds into a dish, I think it's a little spiffy. The ancient Romans, who called almonds Greek Nut, must have thought so too. They used to toss almonds over party guests at weddings and births the same way we throw rice at a bride. Almond trees are native to Asia Minor, although by the earliest written history they had spread throughout the Mediterranean basin. The Arabs cultivated the tree extensively, and the Spanish monks brought them to the United States. Almond trees were widely planted in U.S. soil, but flourished only in California which now grows about half of the world crop.

1 egg, lightly beaten
1 tablespoon milk
6 tablespoons flour, divided
6 soft-shell crabs, cleaned
6 tablespoons butter, divided
1 cup orange juice (2 to 3 medium oranges)
1 tablespoon lime juice
1/2 cup water
1 tablespoon honey
1/2 cup slivered almonds
1/2 cup orange sections

Lightly beat the egg in a shallow pan. Stir in the milk. Set aside. Place 4 tablespoons of the flour in another shallow pan.

Batter the cleaned crabs by dipping each crab first in the egg mixture, then into the flour. Shake off any excess batter and set aside.

To saute the battered crabs, melt 3 tablespoons of the butter in a heavy skillet over low heat. Increase the heat slightly and saute the crabs until done, about 5 minutes on each side, depending on the heat used. As each crab is cooked, drain on absorbent paper and hold in a heated oven.

Make an amandine sauce by adding the remaining butter to the pan juices in the skillet used to saute the crabs. When the butter has melted, stir in the remaining flour, a little at a time. Stir constantly and break up any lumps that form. Continue cooking and stirring for 3 minutes. Add the orange juice, lime juice, water, and honey. Stir until the honey is completely dissolved.

Reduce the heat and simmer for 5 minutes. Add the almonds and orange sections and stir until they are thoroughly coated with the sauce.

To serve the crabs, prepare a bed of cooked rice. Place the crabs on the rice and pour the amandine sauce over all. Serve immediately.

Yield: 6 servings

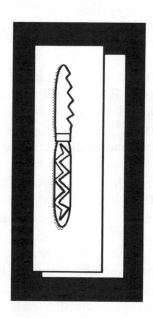

Tomatillo Relish for Grilled Soft-Shell Crab

Tomatillo relish makes a welcome summer accompaniment for the May/September soft-shell season—cool without being bland. It has an extra advantage—it can be made the day before and refrigerated, leaving your time free for your guests.

2/3 pound tomatillos
1 tablespoon olive oil
1/3 cup red wine vinegar
1 tablespoon chopped fresh parsley
1 small tomato, chopped
1 mild chili, chopped
2 teaspoon Pickapeppa Sauce
1/2 teaspoon pepper blend (see page 131)
1/4 teaspoon salt

To make the relish, husk the tomatillos. Divide the tomatillos into four equal portions.

Place two of the tomatillo portions in a blender or food processor and puree. Set aside.

Finely chop one portion of the tomatillos. Set aside.

Finely chop the final portion of the tomatillos, then add to a heavy skillet along with 1 tablespoon olive oil. Heat on medium, and saute the tomatillos for 3 minutes, stirring frequently. Add the red wine vinegar and the remaining ingredients and continue to simmer for an additional 10 minutes. Stir frequently.

Combine the tomatillo puree, chopped tomatillos, and sauteed tomatillos. Refrigerate overnight before serving.

Yield: about 1 cup

Pesto Sauce for Grilled Soft-Shell Crab

This is an unusual combination of ingredients that works flavor magic when served with grilled soft-shells. I serve it in a small bowl on the side. The sauce is a little hot; to cool leave out some of the jalapeño. If you like heat, try substituting different peppers for variety.

1 tablespoon dry white wine
3 tablespoons walnut oil
1 teaspoon oriental sesame oil
2 tablespoons finely chopped seeded jalapeño peppers
2 tablespoons chopped fresh basil
2 tablespoons chopped fresh parsley
1 clove garlic
1 tablespoon grated fresh ginger
1/2 teaspoon salt
1 teaspoon pepper blend (see page 131)

To make the pesto sauce, combine the ingredients in a blender or food processor. Reduce to a paste. Serve chilled or at room temperature.

Yield: slightly more than 1/2 cup

Crab Cakes

Simple Crab Cakes

Crab Cakes

A proper crab cake is just plain good food. Crab cakes linger in memory long after their taste has faded from the palate. And they are versatile. Crab cakes can be made small or large. They can be made with few ingredients or many. They can be eaten with a light sauce or stand alone. Crab cakes are appropriate for breakfast, lunch, or dinner, and may be eaten hot or cold with equal relish. They can be used as a filling for a sandwich, almost in the same manner as a hamburger patty. If you have never made crab cakes, I urge you to try this recipe. I have returned to it again and again.

2 teaspoons flour
1 egg, lightly beaten
1/4 cup light cream
1/4 teaspoon black pepper
1/8 teaspoon salt
2 cups (1 pound) lump crab meat
2 tablespoons butter
2 tablespoons canola or peanut oil

Combine the flour, egg, light cream, pepper, and salt. Stir until the ingredients are blended, then add the crab meat. Stir gently so that the large pieces of crab meat are not broken apart.

Form the mixture into palm-size cakes 1/2 to 3/4 inch thick. Set aside on waxed paper.

In a heavy pan heat 2 tablespoons butter with 2 tablespoons canola or peanut oil. Cook the cakes on medium heat, about 5 minutes each side, until golden brown. Drain on absorbent paper.

Serve hot or cold.

Yield: 4 servings

This recipe gives a moist, light crab cake with a pleasing and unusual set of flavors. The balance of the brandy, lime, and spices is just right.

4 tablespoons butter
3 tablespoons flour
2 1/2 cups milk

4 cups (2 pounds) lump crab meat
1 tablespoon brandy
2 tablespoons minced fresh parsley
1 teaspoon salt
2 tablespoons lime juice
1/2 teaspoon pepper blend (see page 131)
1/4 teaspoon nutmeg
4 eggs, lightly beaten
4 slices dry bread, crushed into fine crumbs
Canola or peanut oil to deep-fry

Melt the butter over low heat. Slowly stir in the flour. Simmer for 5 minutes. Add the milk in a thin stream, stirring constantly. Simmer for 10 minutes.

In a large bowl, combine the crab, white sauce, brandy, parsley, salt, lime juice, pepper blend, and nutmeg. Stir carefully, so that the large chunks of crab meat are not broken. Shape 8 palm-size portions 1/2 to 3/4 inch thick on waxed paper.

Put the lightly beaten egg in a shallow container for dredging. Have the bread crumbs in a dish alongside. Dip each patty into the egg, then roll it in the crumbs. Refrigerate for one hour.

Pour enough oil into a frying pan or wok to cover the crab cakes. Heat the oil to medium-high. Drop the patties into the oil, a few at a time. Fry until golden brown, probably not more than 30 seconds. After frying, drain on absorbent paper.

Yield: 4 servings

Newport Crab Cakes

Betty Shaw gave me this recipe for crab cakes. It is an old recipe coming down from Betty's mother's family. In old Newport when the richest and most prominent people in America spent their summers on the playground, her family's business was to cater dinners and parties to people who were accustomed to the best and were more than able to pay for it. Later, Betty refined the cooking skills she picked up in the family kitchen by studying at the Trianon Palace Hotel at Versailles, the Cordon Bleu School in London (under Mrs. Epstein), and at the Prue Leith Cooking School in London.

For her crab cakes Betty uses a white sauce binder, made a bit thick. Betty also says that the richer the milk, the richer the crab cake. Her favorite accompaniments are marinara and tartar sauce.

3 tablespoons butter
3 tablespoons flour
1 cup milk
1/8 teaspoon salt
1/4 teaspoon white pepper
1/4 teaspoon of mace or nutmeg (sweeter than mace) *or* 1 tablespoon curry powder

2 cups (1 pound) crab meat
3 tablespoons flour to dredge
1 tablespoon water
1 egg, lightly beaten
3/4 fine bread crumbs (about 1 slice)
1 tablespoon butter
1 tablespoon oil

Melt the butter in a saucepan; add the flour and cook, stirring all the while, until the mixture looks a bit dry at the edges, about 2 to 3 minutes over medium heat. Add the milk gradually, stirring vigorously and cook mixture until quite thick, about another 2 to 3 minutes. Remove from heat, season with salt and pepper, and allow to cool. You can add either the mace or the curry powder at this time.

Stir in the crab meat. When combined, shape the mixture into cakes. These can be prepared and put in the refrigerator covered for several hours.

Dip each cake into the flour and dust off the excess. Add the water to the lightly beaten egg and stir to combine. Dip each crab cake in the egg mixture, then into the bread crumbs. For a soft crust use fresh bread crumbs; for a crisper crust use stale bread.

Melt the butter in a heavy skillet. Add 1 tablespoon of oil and saute the cakes over moderate heat. Since all of the ingredients are cooked, it is only a matter of warming the cakes through and getting a nice brown color on the outside. Drain on absorbent paper.

Serve hot.

Yield: 4 servings

Mace

Crab Avocado Cakes

Annette Reddell Hegen, of the Marine Advisory Service in Port Aransas, Texas, gave me this recipe. Some flavors fit together naturally, and crab meat and avocado make up one fine combination. Use the largest crab pieces you have available.

2 cups (1 pound) crab meat
1 avocado, peeled, stoned, and chopped
1/4 cup finely chopped onions
1 egg, beaten
2 tablespoons margarine
2 tablespoons fresh lemon juice
1 tablespoon Dijon mustard
1 tablespoon chopped fresh dill weed
3/4 cup dry bread crumbs, divided
1/4 cup olive oil

Combine the ingredients except the bread crumbs and olive oil in a mixing bowl. Add 1/4 cup of the bread crumbs to the mixture. Form the mixture into 6 crab meat cakes.

Place the remaining 1/2 cup of bread crumbs in a flat pan or dish. Dredge the cakes in the crumbs and set aside.

Heat the oil in a large, heavy skillet on medium heat. Fry the cakes until golden brown, turning once. Drain on absorbent paper.

Serve hot.

Yield: 4 servings

Deep South Crab Cakes

While researching this book I came across a number of recipes from the Deep South, each with a very interesting touch. I liked this dish for its unusual addition of mashed potatoes.

1 large egg
1/4 teaspoon black pepper
3 or 4 drops Tabasco
3 tablespoons minced fresh chives or green onions
1 cup mashed tomatoes, at room temperature or slightly chilled
1 pound lump crab meat
1/4 cup white flour
Vegetable oil for frying
2 lemons, cut into wedges

In a mixing bowl combine the egg, black pepper, Tabasco, and chives. Add the mashed potatoes and blend thoroughly. Carefully add the crab meat and blend carefully keeping as many of the lumps intact as possible. Form into patties about 1 inch thick. Set on wax paper to dry slightly. Lightly dust the crab cakes with flour. Pour about 1 inch of vegetable oil in a skillet and heat to 350 degrees F. Fry the crab cakes until golden brown, about 2 to 3 minutes per side. Remove and drain on absorbent paper.

Serve immediately with lemon wedges.

Yield: 4 servings

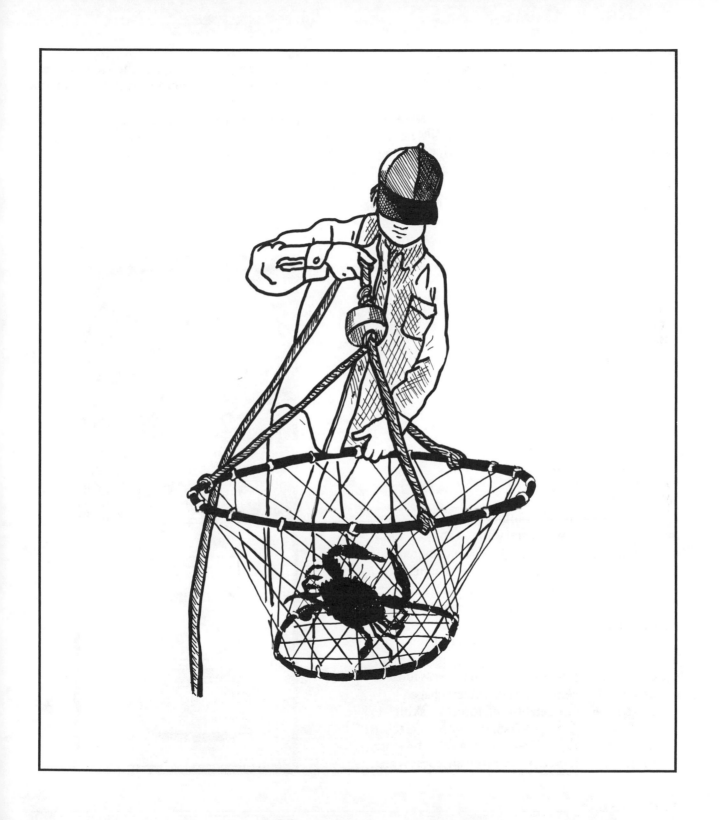

Chesapeake Crab Cakes

There are as many crab cake recipes as there are people on the Chesapeake Bay. Many Chesapeake natives claim to have the only true recipe and some of them will even part with it, minus, of course, the "secret" ingredient. This recipe uses the most basic ingredients commonly found. If you want to claim it has a secret ingredient after you serve it, it is all right with me.

1 large egg
2 tablespoons mayonnaise
1 teaspoon dry mustard
1/2 teaspoon black pepper
2 teaspoons worcestershire
1/2 teaspoon Tabasco
1/4 teaspoon dried basil
1/4 teaspoon dried oregano
1/4 teaspoon dried parsley
1/4 teaspoon paprika
1 pound lump crab meat
1/4 cup bread crumbs
Vegetable oil for frying

In a mixing bowl combine egg, mayonnaise, mustard, pepper, worcestershire, Tabasco, basil, oregano, parsley, and paprika. Blend ingredients until slightly frothy. Place the crab meat in a bowl and pour mixture over the crab. Add the bread crumbs, mixing lightly to avoid breaking up the crab meat lumps.

Form cakes by hand or with an ice cream scoop into 3 to 4 inch rounds about 1 inch thick. Do not pack the cakes too tightly, they should be as loose as possible but firm enough to hold their shape.

Heat enough vegetable oil to cover skillet to about 1/2 to 1 inch deep. When the heat has reached 375 degrees F, fry the crab cakes a few at a time, flipping once until golden brown on all sides. Watch carefully as they cook quickly, about 2 to 3 minutes. Remove with a slotted spoon and drain on absorbent paper.

Serve immediately with slices of lemon, mayonnaise, or other preferred condiments such as hot sauce or mustard. Keep in mind that Chesapeake natives consider it in poor taste to serve crab cakes with ketchup.

Yield: 4 servings

Crab Cakes Caribbeana

This recipe was given to me by Denny Hayes, a self-professed hot food fanatic and lover of anything tropical. It is a dish he enjoyed at the Raintree Restaurant on St. John in the Virgin Islands. While this recipe doesn't equal the depth of heat Denny normally likes, it still has a little bite to it. If you can not find Jamaican allspice, known in Jamaica as pimento, regular ground allspice will substitute. You can also substitute a habañero or serrano pepper for the Scotch bonnet.

Two sauces that I like with Crab Cakes Caribbeana are Red Dipping Sauce (see page 125) and Herb Dipping Sauce (see page 123). Slices of grilled fresh pineapple will also add a nice touch.

1 large egg
1 tablespoon mayonnaise
1/4 teaspoon black pepper
5 to 6 drops Tabasco
1 teaspoon soy sauce
1 tablespoon lime juice
1/8 teaspoon cloves
1/8 teaspoon Jamaican allspice
1/8 teaspoon cayenne
1/2 teaspoon paprika
1/4 teaspoon dry mustard
1/4 teaspoon celery salt
1 Scotch bonnet pepper
1 pound lump crab meat
1/4 cup corn meal or dry bread crumbs
Vegetable oil for frying
Lemon or lime slices, for garnish

Combine all of the ingredients from the egg to the celery salt.

Seed and mince the Scotch bonnet pepper very finely. A note of caution: the Scotch bonnet is considered to be the hottest known edible pepper. Take care not to touch your eyes when handling it. Only a very slight bit of Scotch bonnet juice in or around your eyes can cause a painful and lingering burning sensation. Thorough washing of your hands is a good idea.

Combine the minced pepper with the other ingredients. Add the crab meat and corn meal and blend well. Using your hands or an ice cream scoop, form 8 to 10 patties about 1 inch thick. They should be firm enough to hold their shape but not too compacted. If the mixture feels too loose, add a little more corn meal. Place on wax paper and allow to dry slightly.

Pour the oil into a non-aluminum skillet to about 1 inch depth. Heat oil to 350 degrees F.

Fry the crab cakes a few at a time without allowing them to touch one another in the skillet. Fry about 1 to 2 minutes on each side, or until golden brown. Remove from the skillet and drain on absorbent paper. Serve immediately with slices of lemon and lime.

Yield: 4 servings

Abby's Crab Cakes with Sherry Cayenne Mayonnaise

Chef Abby Nash, formerly of Abby's Restaurant in Ithaca, New York, has been a source of many fine recipes for me as well as a helpful advisor on cooking with crab. The Sherry Cayenne Mayonnaise is a re-creation of a sauce served to Abby at the Fog City Diner. The sauce has a pleasant tangy taste that becomes hotter as the sauce stands.

3 tablespoons butter
1/2 medium onion, diced
1/4 cup celery, diced
1 garlic clove, minced
1/2 teaspoon salt
1/2 teaspoon black pepper
3/4 teaspoon cumin
1 tablespoon minced, fresh parsley
2 eggs
2 tablespoons heavy cream
3 to 4 drops Tabasco
1 tablespoon Dijon mustard
3 tablespoons dry bread crumbs
1 pound crab meat
Butter or oil for frying

Sherry Cayenne Mayonnaise
1 tablespoon dry sherry
1 egg yolk
3/4 teaspoon Dijon smooth mustard
1/4 cup peanut oil
1/4 cup olive oil
1 1/2 teaspoons lemon juice
1/2 teaspoon salt
1/4 teaspoon white pepper
1/8 teaspoon cayenne

To make the crab cakes, heat the butter in a small skillet over low heat. Saute the onions, celery, garlic, salt, pepper, cumin, and parsley until the vegetables are softened. Do not brown. Set aside and let cool.

Mix the eggs, cream, Tabasco, mustard, and crumbs. Add the cooled sauteed mixture and combine. Gently stir in the crab meat. Form the mixture into 1/4 cup balls. Flatten and shape patties 1/2 inch thick.

Melt the butter over medium low heat. Saute until golden brown on both sides, about 5 to 6 minutes in all. Remove from the oil and drain on absorbent paper. Keep warm.

To make the mayonnaise, reduce the sherry by half over low heat. Once the sherry begins to boil it will reduce quickly and will need close attention.

In a small bowl, whisk the yolk and mustard. Slowly add the two oils, a drop at a time at first, whisking constantly. Add the lemon juice, salt, pepper, cayenne, and sherry. Stir together until blended.

Serve the sauce in a boat at the table as a fine accompaniment to the warm crab cakes.

Yield: 6 servings

Stir Fries, Newburgs, Casseroles, etc.

Stir-Fried Crab Meat

As American palates grow steadily more educated, the combination of seafood and oriental seasoning is finding increasing favor. This stir-fry recipe uses five-spice powder, a crucial ingredient that cannot be left out or substituted without changing the dish beyond recognition. Five-spice powder is a blended spice, like curry. It does not have one definitive recipe. This combination is the one I use. If you do not care to make your own five-spice seasoning, it is commonly stocked in oriental markets.

1 tablespoon cornstarch
1/4 cup cool water
2 tablespoons canola oil, divided
1/4 cup mushrooms, thinly sliced
2 tablespoons soy sauce
3 drops oriental sesame oil
2 cups (1 pound) crab meat
2 teaspoons grated fresh ginger root
2 coarsely chopped green onions, tops included
1/8 teaspoon five-spice powder
1 tablespoon dry sherry

Dissolve the cornstarch in the water. Stir until the cornstarch is completely dissolved and no lumps remain. Set aside.

In a wok or skillet, heat 1 tablespoon of the canola oil on low heat. Add the mushrooms and saute 2 minutes. Sprinkle the soy sauce over the mushrooms. Continue to saute, stirring constantly, for an additional 3 minutes.

Increase the heat. Add the remaining canola oil. Stir in the sesame oil, crab meat, ginger, green onions, and five-spice powder. Stir-fry for 2 minutes. Add the sherry and stir to combine.

Reduce the heat. Continuing to stir constantly, add the cornstarch mixture. Stir-fry on low heat for 3 minutes or until the mixture thickens. Serve immediately with or over rice.

Yield: 4 servings

FIVE-SPICE POWDER

3 parts ground star anise
3 parts ground fennel
3 parts ground cinnamon
2 parts ground white pepper
2 parts ground cloves

Fragrant Crab Meat with Rice

Some people seem to think that special tools are needed to prepare an oriental meal. Others, looking at a long list of ingredients, believe that oriental dishes are difficult to make. Neither is true. This dish is prepared using 2 ordinary skillets and a kitchen knife, the same things you would use to prepare fried potatoes. As for difficulty, this dish is simplicity itself. There are only two things to do: fry the rice and saute the crab meat with vegetables. Cooking time is about 30 minutes, less than many cooks spend preparing meat loaf.

Oriental sesame oil
1 cup uncooked rice
2 cups hot water
2 cups (1 pound) crab meat
1/4 cup olive oil
2 tablespoons sherry vinegar
2 tablespoons fresh lime juice
1/2 red bell pepper, finely chopped
1 garlic clove, finely chopped
1 tablespoon finely chopped shallots
1/4 teaspoon black pepper
1 teaspoon salt
1/2 teaspoon five-spice powder (see page 74)

Thinly coat the bottom of a skillet with sesame oil. Fry the rice over medium heat until golden, stirring very frequently. Slowly add 2 cups hot water. Reduce the heat to very low. Cover and cook 20 minutes, or until the rice is done.

In a separate skillet, combine the remaining ingredients. Saute over very low heat 10 minutes, stirring frequently.

Spoon the crab meat mixture over the rice. Serve immediately.

Yield: 4 servings

Sauteed Crab Meat with Wine Sauce

Recipes that can do double duty are always welcome in my kitchen. After a recent dinner party I discovered a small amount of this dish left over. I refrigerated the extra portion. The next evening I reheated what I had saved, and when the mixture was thoroughly heated added enough milk to make it the consistency of medium thick sauce. Spooned over broiled fish, the leftover made a first-rate crab meat sauce. After a quick dusting with paprika, it was ready for the table.

6 tablespoons butter
3 tablespoons flour
2 cups (1 pound) crab meat
1/2 teaspoon salt
4 tablespoons dry white wine
1/2 teaspoon pepper blend (see page 131)
2 teaspoons chopped fresh parsley
2 teaspoons Dijon mustard

Slowly melt the butter in a large, heavy skillet. Add the flour and cook, stirring constantly, for 2 minutes.

Add the remaining ingredients, increase the heat slightly, and cook, stirring frequently, until the mixture has thickened, about 7 minutes. Serve immediately over rice or toast points.

Yield: 4 servings

Southern Crab Jambalaya

This recipe was given to me by a self-professed "home cook." It is based on a southern recipe and is best when accompanied in the finest southern tradition with heaping plates of cornbread. One cornbread I like, the johnny cake, has a name rooted in colonial America. People in those days knew that cornbread fried into a crusty cake kept well on long trips. Also, after frying, the corn cake could be eaten in hand (sort of like a fast-food hamburger) while seated on a horse or wagon. These cakes therefore came to be called journey cakes. During the civil war the name changed slightly and became johnny cake when large numbers of southern soldiers (Johnny Rebs) carried them into battle. I think that johnny cakes go well with this dish, especially when mildly spiced with finely chopped jalapeño peppers. (Incidentially, jambalaya takes its name from the French word for ham, *jambon*.)

2 tablespoons butter
1/4 cup chopped red onion
1/3 cup chopped celery
1 clove garlic, minced
1/4 cup chopped green bell pepper
2 cups chicken stock
1 cup uncooked rice
2 medium tomatoes, chopped
1/2 teaspoon salt
1/4 teaspoon cayenne
1/4 teaspoon white pepper
1/4 teaspoon black pepper
1/8 teaspoon Tabasco
1 tablespoon chopped fresh parsley
1/2 cup cubed, cooked ham
2 cups (1 pound) crab meat

Melt the butter in a heavy pot over low heat. Increase the heat and add the onion, celery, garlic, and green pepper. Saute for 5 minutes. Add the remaining ingredients, except the crab meat, and stir to combine. Bring the liquid to a boil, then cover and simmer for 20 minutes.

Turn off the heat, stir in the crab meat, and let the jambalaya stand in the pot until the liquid is absorbed. Serve hot.

Yield: 6 servings

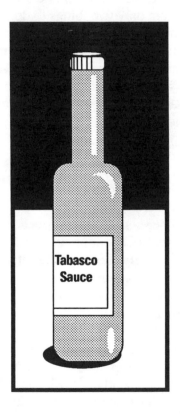

Crab in Caribbean Sweet Pepper Sauce

This is a distinctly Caribbean dish. I like to serve it with baked plantain. To make the plantains, allow about 1 large plantain for 2 servings. Select plantains with spotted yellow coloring, the stage when the plantain has just begun to form its sugars. Cut off each end, but do not peel. Bake 50 minutes at 350 degrees F. Peel, cut into 1/2 inch thick disks and serve hot. Plantains cooked this way are good plain or served with a simple sauce of butter and rum.

1/4 cup olive oil
1/2 green bell pepper, finely chopped
2 tablespoons white wine vinegar
2 tablespoons lime juice
2 large cloves of garlic, very finely chopped
1 teaspoon salt
1/4 teaspoon black pepper
2 cups (1 pound) crab meat

To make the pepper sauce, heat the olive oil on medium heat in a heavy skillet. Add the pepper sauce ingredients and cook for 5 minutes. Reduce the heat to low and cook an additional 20 minutes. Watch the heat carefully, and lower it further if the pan gets too hot.

Add the crab meat, stir to combine, and cook an additional 5 minutes. Serve hot.

Yield: 4 servings

Crab in Brazilian Spiced Sauce

I used a jalapeño pepper in this re-creation of a traditional Brazilian dish. In Brazil they use a slightly different—and much hotter—pepper, one that is seldom seen in U.S. markets. I like to serve this over rice, accompanied with a cool fruit cup or slices of fresh pineapple as counterpoint to the heat of this spicy delight.

2 tablespoons olive oil
1 jalapeño pepper, seeded and finely chopped
1 small tomato, finely chopped
2 cups (1 pound) lump crab meat
1/3 cup dry white wine
1/4 lemon, juice of

Heat the olive oil in a heavy skillet over medium heat. Add the jalapeño pepper, and saute 3 minutes. Add the chopped tomato, and cook an additional 2 minutes.

Stir in the remaining ingredients, reduce the heat to low, and simmer an additional 15 minutes. Stir frequently. Serve hot with rice.

Yield: 4 servings

Crab Meat Flambé

Is it possible to forget a flaming dish meal? I know that I'll never forget the special charm of my first one. The careful preparing of the flaming pan, the gingerly way the chef handled the utensils, and the finale of the yellow blue flame burning over the food shouted that everything about this evening was special. Cook this for your candlelight and wine occasions. It is a treat your guests are sure to enjoy.

3 tablespoons butter
2 shallots, finely chopped
2 cups (1 pound) crab meat
1/4 teaspoon white pepper
2 tablespoons chopped fresh parsley
1/2 cup dry white wine
1/4 cup brandy

Melt the butter in a heavy skillet over low heat. Add the shallots and saute, stirring frequently, for 5 minutes.

Stir in the crab meat. If you are using lump crab meat, stir carefully so that the large crab pieces are not broken apart. Cook an additional 3 minutes, continuing to stir frequently.

Add the pepper, parsley, and white wine. Stir to blend. Heat the mixture thoroughly. Stir in the brandy. Heat the mixture until the brandy is just warm, but do not heat until boiling.

Flame the dish by touching a match to the liquid by the edge of the pan. If the flame is inadequate, warm a tablespoon of brandy and touch a match to the brandy in the tablespoon. Gently pour the flaming brandy into the dish. Allow the brandy to burn itself out.

Serve immediately over rice or lightly buttered toast points.

Yield: 4 servings

Crabs Girardeau Flambé

This is an old family recipe from the Louisiana delta. It was given to me by Arlene and Paul Hodge of Plaquemine. The Hodges do not know the Girardeau who lent his name to this dish. Paul Hodge's mother found the recipe written on the back leaf of an antique cookbook below the notation, "Girardeau's recipe." This impressive and flavorful meal has been a Hodge family favorite since.

3 tablespoons butter
1/2 pound mushrooms, thinly sliced
2 cups (1 pound) crab meat
1 jigger brandy
1 1/2 cups light cream
1/4 teaspoon black pepper
1 tablespoon chopped fresh parsley

Using a chafing dish, melt the butter. Increase the heat under the chafing dish and stir in the sliced mushrooms. Cook, stirring frequently, for 8 to 10 minutes.

Add the crab meat and stir to combine. If you are using lump crab meat, stir gently to avoid breaking the large pieces of crab. Heat the crab meat thoroughly.

Stir in the brandy. Heat the mixture until the brandy is just warm, but do not heat until boiling.

Flame the dish by touching a match to the liquid by the edge of the pan. If the flame is inadequate, warm a tablespoon of brandy and touch a match to the brandy in the tablespoon. Gently pour the flaming brandy into the dish.

Allow the brandy to burn itself out. When it is extinguished, stir in the cream. Sprinkle the crab mixture with pepper and parsley. Continue to cook for 4 minutes.

Serve immediately, either over or with rice.

Yield: 4 servings

Crab Meat à la King

This elegant recipe is another of the rich preparations originating in the kitchen of Lorenzo Delmonico, the premier restaurateur of New York's Gilded Age. He named a new crab dish à la Keene after one of his customers who suggested it. The name soon evolved to à la king and the basic preparation was applied to seafood as well as to chicken.

2 tablespoons butter
1 tablespoon very finely chopped celery
1 tablespoon flour
1/2 teaspoon salt
1/4 teaspoon pepper blend (see page 131)
1/2 teaspoon chopped fresh parsley
1 cup heavy cream
2 hard-boiled eggs, finely chopped
1 tablespoon finely cut chives
2 cups (1 pound) crab meat
1/4 cup dry sherry
Paprika

Using a heavy skillet, slowly melt the butter over low heat. Add the celery and cook, stirring frequently, for 5 minutes.

Add the flour a little at a time, stirring constantly, to form a smooth mixture. With the back of a wooden spoon, break apart any lumps that form. Add the salt, pepper blend, and parsley. Mix thoroughly.

Blend in the cream. Cook on low until mixture begins to thicken, about 6 to 8 minutes. Stir frequently. Do not allow it to burn on the bottom.

Add the eggs, chives, and crab meat. Cook an additional minute to heat thoroughly, stirring constantly. Add the sherry and gently stir.

Serve immediately over lightly buttered toast. Sprinkle with paprika.

Yield: 4 servings

Crab Newburg

The newburg style of presenting seafood is a uniquely American innovation from the period following the first flowering of the industrial revolution. It originated in the New York kitchen of Lorenzo Delmonico, the ranking restaurateur of his day. It was quickly picked up (Mr. Delmonico reportedly said stolen) by Fred Harvey, the railroad dining-car czar. Soon cross-country travelers were eating newburg dishes at $1.00 per meal. The cost was far above anything seen before, but so was the quality of the food. It firmly established seafood newburgs in the galaxy of American classics.

1/3 cup butter
2 tablespoons flour
2 cups light cream
4 beaten egg yolks
2 cups (1 pound) crab meat
2 teaspoons lemon juice
1/4 teaspoon mace
1 teaspoon Pickapeppa Sauce
1/2 teaspoon salt

Melt the butter over low heat. Add the flour a little at a time, and simmer for 5 minutes, stirring constantly.

Reduce the heat and stir in the cream, cooking slowly until thick, about 7 minutes. Pour the egg yolks into the mixture, stirring constantly, and cook 1 to 2 minutes. Stir in the crab meat, lemon juice, mace, Pickapeppa Sauce, and salt. Cook an additional minute to heat thoroughly.

Add the sherry and stir to blend. Sprinkle with paprika. Serve over lightly buttered toast.

Yield: 6 servings

Crab Supreme

Make this delicious dish for your most honored guests. The flaming presentation is impressive and the taste will leave them hungry for more.

1/4 cup butter
1/4 cup flour
1 cup dry white wine
2 tablespoons dry vermouth
1 teaspoon dry mustard
1/4 teaspoon pepper blend (see page 131)
1/2 cup chicken stock
1/4 cup light cream
1/4 cup clarified butter
2 teaspoons lemon juice
3 tablespoons butter
4 cups (2 pounds) crab meat
1/4 cup brandy

Slowly melt the 1/4 cup butter in a saucepan. Add the flour, increase the heat slightly, and cook for 5 minutes, stirring constantly. Add the wine and vermouth, then simmer an additional 5 minutes. Stir in the mustard, pepper blend, and chicken stock. Simmer until the mixture thickens, about 8 to 10 minutes. Stir in the cream and clarified butter. Set aside, but keep warm.

Slowly melt the 3 tablespoons butter in a heavy skillet. Add the crab meat and lemon juice, then increase the heat to moderate. Cook the crab, stirring constantly and rapidly until the crab is thoroughly warm. Stir in the brandy. When the brandy is just warm, remove from the heat. Flame the brandy by touching a match to the liquid by the edge of the pan. If the flame is inadequate, warm a tablespoon of brandy and touch a match to the brandy in the tablespoon. Gently pour the flaming brandy into the dish. Allow the brandy to burn out. When it is extinguished, add the wine-chicken stock mixture and gently stir.

Yield: 8 servings

Northwest Crab Delight

David Church is a fellow cookbook author who spends time on both the Atlantic and Pacific coasts. Over the years he has collected a knockout recipe file, and this is one of his best.

1 1/2 sticks butter, divided
1/4 cup all-purpose flour
3 cups milk
1 pound Swiss cheese, chopped or shredded
1 tablespoon salt
1/4 teaspoon white pepper
1/4 teaspoon dry mustard
3 tablespoons lemon juice
1 to 1 1/2 cups cooked crab meat or crab meat
   combined with shrimp
1/2 cup cream sherry
2 to 3 garlic cloves, peeled and minced
1 green bell pepper, chopped
1 red bell or yellow bell pepper, chopped
1 cup sliced mushrooms
Paprika or parsley, for garnish

Reserve 2 tablespoons of the butter. Melt the rest over low heat in a saucepan. Add the flour and stir. Add the milk and stir. Add the cheese and cook until the cheese is melted. Add the salt, pepper, mustard, and lemon. Add the seafood and sherry and blend. Lower the heat.

Place the reserved 2 tablespoons butter in a small skillet and melt over low heat. Saute the garlic, then add the peppers and mushrooms. Saute until they are soft. Combine them with the seafood mixture. Dust with paprika or minced fresh parsley.

Yield: 6 to 8 servings

Tropical Crab Meat Curry

Here is a recipe I re-created from a meal I was served on Dominica, the last really unspoiled island in the Caribbean. Food on Dominica is as authentically Caribbean as it gets. If you can't go there but want to duplicate the tropical flavor of the islands in your own kitchen, use the freshest vegetables and crab meat possible and don't forget the lime. Mango chutney is a fine accompaniment for this curry.

1 large onion, finely chopped
2 carrots, finely chopped
1/4 green bell pepper, sliced in very thin strips
1 stalk celery, finely chopped, leaves and all
2 small tomatoes, chopped
1/4 teaspoon salt
Grated zest of 1/4 lime
Water to cover
1 tablespoon butter
2 cups (1 pound) crab meat
1 1/2 teaspoons curry powder
1 1/2 tablespoons flour
1 1/2 tablespoons water

Place the onion, carrots, green pepper, celery, tomatoes, salt, and lime zest in a large heavy skillet. Cover with water and bring to a rapid boil. Reduce the heat and simmer 2 hours, until you have a paste-like consistency. Stir frequently.

Add the butter to the skillet. As the butter melts, stir to combine. Add the crab meat. Stir to combine and cook 3 minutes. Stir in the curry powder.

In a mixing bowl, make a paste of the flour and water. Add to the mixture in the skillet and stir. Simmer 10 minutes, stirring frequently. Serve over rice, with mango chutney on the side.

Yield: 4 servings

Simple Crab Curry

This simple curry recipe was given to me by Charles Watson, who picked it up while in military service in India. The curry powder blend is his too, given to me with the cautionary note that grinding the spices just before use makes a big difference in the flavor.

2 tablespoons butter
1 tablespoon chopped green bell pepper
1 tablespoon mango chutney
1/2 teaspoon curry powder
2 cups (1 pound) crab meat
Cooked rice

Melt the butter in a heavy skillet over low heat. Increase the heat and add the green pepper. Saute 5 minutes. Add the chutney, curry powder, and crab meat. Saute, stirring constantly, for 3 minutes. Serve hot with either brown or white rice.

Yield: 4 servings

CURRY POWDER

5 parts ground turmeric
4 parts ground coriander
3 parts ground cayenne
2 parts ground cumin
2 parts ground black pepper
1 part ground cloves
1 part ground ginger

Crab Meat au Gratin

There are many versions of this famous recipe. Some offer a long list of ingredients and some the bare minimium. Some are extremely complex and others are simple. I think that this recipe achieves all of the flavor and complexity of this wonderful dish with the least possible effort and time. It seems to me to fit Albert Einstein's dictum that all things should be made as simple as possible, but not one bit simpler.

3 tablespoons butter
2 tablespoons flour
2 cups milk

2 tablespoons butter
1/3 clove garlic, sliced
1 cup sliced mushrooms
2 tablespoons soy sauce
1/4 teaspoon black pepper
2 cups (1 pound) crab meat
1/4 cup grated sharp cheddar cheese
1/4 cup grated Swiss cheese
1/2 teaspoon worcestershire
1/8 teaspoon Tabasco
2 tablespoons chicken stock
1/4 teaspoon salt
1/2 teaspoon white pepper
1/3 cup fine dry bread crumbs (about 1 slice)

To make the white sauce, melt the 3 tablespoons butter over low heat. Slowly stir in the flour. Simmer on low heat for 5 minutes. Add the milk in a thin, steady stream, stirring constantly. Simmer an additional 10 minutes.

Preheat the oven to 400 degrees F.

Melt 2 tablespoons butter in a large, heavy skillet over low heat. Add the sliced garlic and saute 3 minutes, stirring frequently. Discard the garlic. Add the mushrooms to the skillet. Saute 2 minutes, then sprinkle with the soy sauce and stir to combine. Continuing to stir, saute the mushrooms. Add the pepper and cook 4 minutes.

Add the white sauce, crab meat, grated cheddar, grated Swiss, worcestershire, Tabasco, chicken stock, salt, white pepper and bread crumbs. Stir thoroughly. Pour into a lightly greased oven-proof baking dish. Bake uncovered for 25 to 30 minutes and serve.

Yield: 6 servings

Crab Mornay

The first time I made this dish, my reaction the next day was to make it again. And I did. I think this is one you'll come back to.

1/2 cup (1 stick) butter
1/2 cup flour
1 small bunch green onions, chopped
1/2 cup finely chopped fresh parsley
1 pint half-and-half
3/4 pound grated Swiss cheese
2 cups (1 pound) crab meat
1/8 teaspoon nutmeg
1/4 teaspoon salt
1/4 teaspoon pepper blend (see page 131)
1/8 teaspoon cayenne
1 tablespoon dry sherry
1 tablespoon butter
3/4 cup fresh bread crumbs (about 1 slice)

Preheat the oven to 350 degrees F.

Melt the stick of butter in a heavy skillet over low heat. Add the flour slowly, stirring constantly, to make a smooth sauce. Break apart any lumps that form in the sauce. Increase the heat slightly, and cook 5 minutes, continuing to stir constantly. Add the onions and parsley. Cook an additional 5 minutes. Slowly pour in the half-and-half, stirring as you pour. Add the grated cheese and simmer, stirring, until the cheese is completely melted. Add the crab meat, nutmeg, salt, pepper blend, and cayenne to the cheese sauce. Pour the mixture into a lightly greased oven-proof baking dish. In a separate saucepan, melt 1 tablespoon butter slowly. Toss with the fresh bread crumbs. Set aside. Sprinkle the buttered bread crumbs over the top. Bake uncovered for 45 minutes. Stir in the sherry and serve.

Yield: 4 servings

Crab Casserole Richmond

I was given this recipe several years ago while visiting friends in Richmond, Virginia. The old family recipe had vague directions of the most charming sort. Having seen the original copy, I really don't know how my friends got from there to here, but the results speak for themselves.

1/4 cup butter
1/3 cup finely chopped celery
1/3 cup finely chopped onions
1/3 cup finely chopped green bell pepper
1/4 cup flour
2 cups milk
2 cups (1 pound) crab meat
1 tablespoon brandy
2 teaspoons worcestershire
1/2 teaspoon dry mustard
1/4 teaspoon black pepper
1/4 teaspoon salt
1 tablespoon dry basil
1 tablespoon butter
3/4 cup fresh bread crumbs (about 1 slice)

Preheat the oven to 350 degrees F. Melt the butter in a heavy skillet over low heat. Add the vegetables. Increase the heat, and saute for 5 minutes, stirring frequently. Add the flour a little at a time, stirring constantly. Add the milk in a thin stream, continuing to stir constantly. Cook the mixture until just boiling, then simmer. Add the remaining ingredients, except for the the bread crumbs and 1 tablespoon butter. Pour into a greased baking dish.

In a saucepan, melt the butter slowly. Toss with the bread crumbs. Sprinkle the bread crumbs over the top of the casserole and bake for 30 minutes.

Yield: 4 servings

Crab Florentine Casserole

This is a marvelous recipe, but you will cheat yourself if you use anything less than very fresh, crisp spinach. You need about a pound and a half of fresh spinach to get the 2 cups of cooked spinach called for. After cooking the spinach, you cannot chop it too finely.

1 cup evaporated milk
1/2 cup mild cheddar cheese, cubed
1/4 teaspoon pepper blend (see page 131)
1/8 teaspoon Tabasco
1/4 cup chopped red bell pepper
1/8 teaspoon curry powder

2 cups chopped, cooked spinach
2 cups (1 pound) crab meat

Preheat the oven to 350 degrees F.
To prepare the cheese sauce, heat the milk in a saucepan over low heat. Add the cheese and cook, stirring constantly, until the cheese has melted and the mixture is smooth. Add the spices and red pepper and stir until blended. Set aside over warm heat.
To make the dish, arrange the cooked spinach on the bottom of a lightly greased baking dish. Spoon the crab meat over the spinach. Top with the cheese sauce. Bake until lightly brown and serve.

Yield: 6 servings

Simple Deviled Crab

Deviled crab doesn't get any simpler than this, and it can be baked in crab shells, ramekins, or a casserole dish. Bring a large pot of water to a rapid boil if you have crab shells. Add 1 teaspoon of baking soda for each crab shell. Select large crab shells. Discard any shells with cracks. Scrub the shells with a stiff brush until clean. Drop into the boiling water. Boil 25 minutes. Remove from the pot, rinse in cool water, and set aside to dry.

1/4 cup butter
1 cup milk
2 cups dry bread crumbs (about 6 slices), divided
2 cups (1 pound) crab meat
1/2 teaspoon salt
1/4 teaspoon black pepper
1/8 teaspoon cayenne

Preheat the oven to 375 degrees F.
Melt the butter in a small saucepan over low heat. Set aside, but keep warm.
Pour the milk into a small mixing bowl. Reserving 1/4 cup of the bread crumbs, add the remaining 1 3/4 cups to the milk and allow to soak.
Combine all of the ingredients except the reserved bread crumbs Stir until thoroughly combined.
Stuff the deviled crab mixture into crab shell or a lightly greased baking dish. Bake for 30 minutes and serve immediately.

Yield: 4 servings

Mobile Bay Stuffed Crab

This recipe was told to me by Alice Knox, a cook who grew up on the shores of Mobile Bay and really knows her business. She told me I could put it in any form I wanted to as long as I told it her way too. Here is the way Ms. Knox gave this recipe to me: "You chop up all the meat real fine. Put that in a pan with the crumbs from 2 slices of toast that you've pulled all apart. Put in about a good tablespoon of finely chopped tomato and a tablespoon of butter. Squeeze half a lemon over it real good. Grate up just a little of the lemon rind and put that in there too. Put a big thick pinch of parsley and a little pinch of nutmeg and one of red pepper. Heat it all up together real good. Put that all back in the crab shell. Put a dab of butter on top and bake it about 300 degrees F for 15 or 20 minutes." After a bit of translating, here it is.

1 tablespoon butter
2 cups (1 pound) crab meat, shredded
2/3 cup toast crumbs (about 2 slices)
1 1/2 tablespoons finely chopped tomato
1 teaspoon chopped fresh parsley
1/4 teaspoon nutmeg
1/8 teaspoon cayenne
1 teaspoon grated lemon zest
1/2 lemon, juice of
Butter, softened

Preheat the oven to 300 degrees F.

In a heavy skillet, melt the butter over low heat. Add the crab meat, crumbs, tomato, parsley, nutmeg and cayenne. Stir and cook 3 minutes. Stir in the lemon zest. Sprinkle the lemon juice over the mixture and stir. Remove from the heat and stuff the mixture into crab shells. Spread a thin layer of softened butter over the stuffing mix in each crab shell.

Arrange the crab shells on a cookie sheet. Bake for 15 to 20 minutes, until golden brown and serve.

Yield: 4 servings

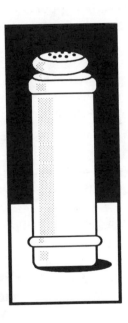

Stuffed Blue Crab

This spicy recipe was developed to use the claw meat of the blue crab. You can also use the meat from other parts of other crabs. The color and taste may be slightly different, but it will still be delicious.

2 slices bacon
1/2 cup finely chopped onion
1/2 cup finely chopped celery
1/4 cup finely chopped green bell pepper
1 clove garlic minced
2 cups crushed cracker crumbs
1 teaspoon dry mustard
1/4 teaspoon salt
2 tablespoons chopped fresh parsley
1/8 teaspoon cayenne pepper
2 cups (1 pound) crab claw meat or other crab meat
1 egg, beaten
1/4 cup milk
1/2 cup butter, melted
1 teaspoon worcestershire

Preheat the oven to 350 degrees F.

Begin the stuffing mix by frying the bacon in a heavy skillet until crisp. Remove the bacon, leaving the grease in the skillet. Crumble the bacon into small bits and reserve.

Add the onions, celery, green pepper, and garlic to the skillet with the bacon grease. Saute the vegetables over low heat for 8 minutes.

Combine the cracker crumbs, mustard, salt, parsley, and cayenne. Add the crab meat, egg, milk, melted butter, and worcestershire. Add the sauteed vegetables. Stir until well blended.

Stuff the mixture into crab shells, ramekins, or a casserole dish. Bake for 25 minutes or until golden brown and serve.

Yield: 6 servings

Southern Deviled Crabs

I think this is a recipe you will return to again and again. It is a re-creation of the deviled crabs I ate in Florida, but I have had similar crabs all along the Gulf coast and up the Atlantic seaboard. A dish like this is too good to stay in one place very long.

2 tablespoons butter
2 tablespoons flour
1/2 cup milk
2 cups (1 pound) crab meat
1/2 teaspoon prepared mustard
2 teaspoons chopped fresh parsley
1 teaspoon worcestershire
1/8 teaspoon Tabasco
1/4 teaspoon salt
1/2 teaspoon black pepper
1 egg, lightly beaten
2 teaspoons butter
2 tablespoons dry bread crumbs, finely crushed

Preheat the oven to 350 degrees F.

Melt 2 tablespoons of butter in a heavy skillet over low heat. Add the flour slowly, stirring constantly, to make a smooth sauce. Break apart any lumps that form in the sauce. Continuing to stir, add the milk in a thin stream. Increase the heat slightly, and cook 8 minutes.

Add the crab meat and stir. Add the mustard, parsley, worcestershire, Tabasco, salt, and pepper. Cook for 4 minutes, stirring frequently. Add the lightly beaten egg and stir. Remove from the heat.

Melt 2 teaspoons butter in a small pan. Add the dry bread crumbs and stir to coat. Set aside.

Stuff the deviled crab mixture into crab shells, ramekins, or a casserole dish. Top with the buttered bread crumbs. Bake for 30 minutes or until browned, and serve.

Yield: 4 servings

Deviled Crabs Rhonda

I like deviled crabs that blend traditional flavors with a peppery nip. This is my favorite deviled crab recipe. I serve it with green salad and toast lightly brushed with olive oil.

1/4 cup butter
1/2 clove garlic, quartered
1/2 cup chopped onion
1/2 cup chopped green pepper
3 cups (1 1/2 pounds) crab meat
3/4 cup soft bread crumbs (about 1 slice)
1/4 cup milk
1 1/2 tablespoons Dijon mustard
1 1/2 teaspoons Pickapeppa Sauce
1/8 lemon, juice of
1/2 teaspoon salt
1/4 teaspoon Tabasco
1/4 teaspoon white pepper
Paprika

Prepare the crab shells (see page 84).
Preheat the oven to 350 degrees F.
Melt the butter in a heavy skillet over low heat. Add the garlic, celery and green pepper. Increase the heat, and saute for 5 minutes, stirring frequently. Remove from the heat. Discard the garlic.

Combine all of the ingredients except the paprika. Spoon the deviled crab meat into prepared crab shells or a lightly greased oven-proof baking dish. Dust with the paprika. Bake at 350 degrees F uncovered for 25 minutes and serve.

Yield: 6 servings as a first course, 3 as a main course

Crab Fettuccine Supreme

I welcome the taste and aroma of Italian cuisine. This dish, rich with the flavor of Mediterranean ingredients, has a fresh, clear taste. The better the tomatoes, the better your sauce will turn out. My choice of tomatoes for this recipe is freshly ripened plum tomatoes, sometimes called Roma tomatoes. If you cannot get good, fresh tomatoes, use canned tomatoes and reduce the simmering time in the first step to 25 minutes.

Water to cover the bottom of a pot
2 pounds tomatoes, sliced in quarters lengthways
2 green onions, finely chopped
1/4 teaspoon salt
1/4 teaspoon garlic powder
1/2 teaspoon pepper blend (see page 131)
3 tablespoons chopped fresh parsley, divided
1/4 cup olive oil
2 cups (1 pound) crab meat
3 tablespoons dry white wine
1 pound cooked fettuccine

Thinly cover the bottom of a pot with water. Add the tomatoes, onions, salt, garlic powder, pepper blend, and 2 tablespoons of the parsley. Cover and simmer, stirring occasionally, for 45 minutes.

Remove the sauce from the heat and puree in a food processor. Return to the heat, add the remaining parsley, and cook an additional 10 minutes.

Add the olive oil and stir until the oil is thoroughly blended with the tomato mixture. Stir in the crab meat and wine. Stir, and heat thoroughly. Spoon over the pasta and serve.

Yield: 6 servings

Crab Meat Manicotti with Tomato Sauce

I developed this recipe as a stuffing for manicotti shells, but it can also be used with lasagne noodles. For lasagne, cook 16 lasagne noodles and lay them flat on your counter. Divide the cooked crab meat and spinach mixture into 16 equal portions. Place one portion of the mixture on each noodle and roll up. To hold the rolls together it may be necessary to tie each with a string. Arrange the lasagne noodles in a baking dish as you would the manicotti and continue with the recipe.

2 tablespoons olive oil
1 tablespoon finely chopped onion
1 clove garlic, sliced in halves
1 pound cooked tomatoes, finely chopped
1/2 teaspoon pepper blend (see page 131)
1 tablespoon chopped fresh basil

1 1/2 cups uncooked spinach
1/8 teaspoon allspice
1 cup (1/2 pound) crab meat
8 cooked manicotti shells
1 tablespoon butter
2 tablespoons chopped shallots
Parmesan cheese

To prepare the tomato sauce, heat the olive oil in a heavy skillet over medium low heat. Add the onion and garlic. Saute for 4 minutes. Discard the garlic. Add the remaining tomato sauce ingredients, reduce heat, and simmer, covered, for 30 minutes, stirring frequently. Set aside over warm heat.

Preheat the oven to 400 degrees F.

Chop the spinach finely. Boil the spinach in a little water with the allspice until the spinach leaves are limp. Drain, then combine the spinach mixture with the crab meat until thoroughly combined.

Melt the butter in a heavy skillet over low heat and add the shallots. Saute until tender, about 5 minutes. Reduce the heat to very low. Add the crab and spinach mixture and cook until heated, stirring continuously. Remove from the heat.

To make the dish, divide the crab meat and spinach mixture into 8 equal portions. Stuff each of the manicotti shells with as much of the mixture as it will hold. Reserve any additional crab meat mixture.

Brush the bottom of a baking dish lightly with the tomato sauce. Arrange the stuffed manicotti shells in the baking dish. Stir any additional crab meat mixture into the sauce. Pour the sauce over the pasta shells. Dust with the Parmesan cheese.

Bake for 25 minutes and serve hot.

Serve immediately.

Yield: 4 servings

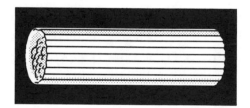

Southwestern Crab Meat Enchiladas

This southwestern entree takes a bit of preparation, but the results more than justify the time. I re-created this recipe from a meal I was served in the Espanola Valley region of New Mexico. Whether entertaining guests or rewarding yourself with something extra special, you will find this blend of Sante Fe with the seashore is just the thing. I serve these enchiladas with Spanish rice, guacamole, chips with queso sauce, and jalapeño nachos.

1/2 cup butter, divided
1/4 cup + 2 tablespoons chopped red bell pepper, divided
1/4 cup + 2 tablespoons chopped green bell pepper, divided
1/4 cup minced shallots
2 jalapeño chili pods, seeded
1 garlic clove
1 teaspoon dried oregano
1/2 teaspoon cumin
1/4 teaspoon pepper blend (see page 131)
1 cup heavy cream
1/4 cup dry vermouth
2 cups grated Monterey jack cheese
1 cup grated sharp cheddar
1/2 cup sour cream
1/2 cup chopped green onions, including tops
3 tomatoes, small
2 cups (1 pound) crab meat
Paprika

12 flour tortillas

Using a large, heavy skillet, melt half of the butter over low heat. Add 1/4 cup red bell peppers, 1/4 cup green bell peppers, the shallots, jalapeños, garlic, and oregano. Increase the heat slightly and cook 6 minutes, stirring frequently. Stir in the cumin and pepper blend.

Add the heavy cream and dry vermouth. Bring to a boil, stirring constantly. Immediately reduce the heat, continuing to stir constantly. Simmer 3 minutes.

Mix the Monterey jack and cheddar cheese. Add half the cheese to the mixture. Stir until completely melted. Remove from the heat and stir in the sour cream.

In a separate skillet, melt the other half of the butter over low heat. Add the green onions and tomatoes, increase the heat slightly, and cook 3 minutes. Reduce heat. Pour half of the cream sauce into the skillet with the sauteed onions and tomatoes. Add the crab meat. Stir to combine. Cook 1 minute or until thoroughly heated.

Preheat the oven to 375 degrees F.

Lay out the tortillas for filling. Spoon the crab meat and cream mixture into the tortillas, rolling each one as it is made. Transfer each completed enchilada into a shallow, lightly greased baking dish. Arrange the enchiladas so that the finished seam is facing down in the dish.

When all of the enchiladas are in the baking dish, pour the remaining cream sauce over all. Cover the dish and bake for 25 minutes. Remove the enchiladas from the oven. Sprinkle the remaining cheese over the enchiladas, then top with the remaining 2 tablespoons each of red and green bell peppers. Finish by dusting with paprika and serve.

Yield: 6 servings

Crab Crepes with Sour Cream

This recipe offers the delicious combination of crab meat, sour cream, and white wine. Before modern refrigeration sour cream was added to food to keep from wasting cream that had soured. The slightly acidic flavor proved so popular that it became a regular ingredient in a vast array of dishes— fish, meat, pasta, poultry, and vegetables.

Crepe Batter
4 eggs
1 1/2 cups flour, sifted
2 cups milk
1 tablespoon butter

Crab Meat Filling
1/4 cup dry white wine
1 teaspoon finely chopped shallots
1 tablespoon chopped fresh parsley
1/4 cup butter
2 tablespoons flour
1/2 cup sour cream
1 cup (1/2 pound) crab meat

To prepare the crepe batter, sift the flour into a mixing bowl. Lightly beat the eggs. Melt the butter over low heat. Stir the milk and the melted butter into the beaten eggs. Gradually combine the egg-milk mixture with the flour, beating with a wire whisk until the batter is smooth. Do not allow any lumps to remain. Cover this mixture, refrigerate, and allow to stand for at least an hour before using; if you use the batter immediately, the tenderness of the crepe will suffer. The batter should thicken as it ages. If the batter becomes too thick, thin the mixture by adding milk, a teaspoon or two at a time, and stirring thoroughly. The batter should have the consistency of heavy cream, with just enough body to evenly coat a large spoon.

If you do not want to make your crepe batter from scratch, remember that a crepe is really just a thin pancake. If you will look on the sides of the pancake mix boxes at your grocer's, some of the brands (such as Aunt Jemima's) will explain how to adapt their mix for use as crepe batter.

To cook the crepes, select a heavy skillet, preferably one with sloping sides. If the skillet has been specifically designed for crepe making, so much the better. Lightly grease the skillet with butter, then heat the pan until it is hot but not smoking. A good, even temperature is important. If you find the skillet getting too hot, remove the pan from the heat and wave it around until the temperature cools a bit. The proper temperature is important for the cooking of each crepe.

Lift the skillet off the heat and pour in 2 tablespoons of the batter. Tip the pan from side to side in a circular motion to coat the cooking surface with a very thin layer of batter. This is a test crepe. The batter should spread and set evenly on the pan. Adjust the amount of batter for each crepe as needed. If the batter is too thick, you may need to thin the batter as instructed above.

Cook each crepe over a medium heat until the bottom is lightly browned, about one minute. Gently lift on edge of the crepe to see the underside. The bottom should be lightly but evenly browned. Flip the crepe and cook for about 30 seconds. You can flip with your fingers, if you are careful. The second side of the crepe will brown much less evenly than the first side; this is to be expected. (Later this less attractive side will form the inside of the crepe.) When the crepe has been cooked, set it aside, and repeat, stacking the crepes between layers of waxed paper.

Crepes can be made days or even weeks ahead of time and reheated before serving. (This means that if you burn or mess up a crepe you have plenty of time to get rid of the evidence.) Crepes keep well for at least 48 hours wrapped in plastic wrap and stored in the refrigerator. Crepes can be kept for several weeks by sealing in plastic and freezing. When freezing or refrigerating the crepes, separate them with waxed paper.

To prepare the crab meat filling, combine the wine, shallots, and parsley in a saucepan and bring to a boil. Reduce the heat, and simmer for 3 minutes. Add the butter and cook until melted. Stir in the flour, breaking apart any lumps that form in the sauce. Simmer for 5 minutes. Add the sour cream and stir to combine. Remove from the heat. Reserve 1/3 of the sauce.

Return the remaining 2/3 of the sauce to the heat. Add the crab meat and bring the mixture to a boil. Remove the crab meat filling from the heat.

Preheat the oven to 375 degrees F.

To assemble the crepes, divide the filling mixture into 12 equal parts. Place each crepe on a piece of the waxed paper so that the rich, golden brown hue of the side of the crepe cooked first is down. Spoon one of the twelve equal portions of filling mixture onto each crepe. Roll the crepes into cylinders. Cover cover the crepes with the reserved sauce. Bake for 5 minutes and serve.

Yield: 6 servings of 2 crepes each

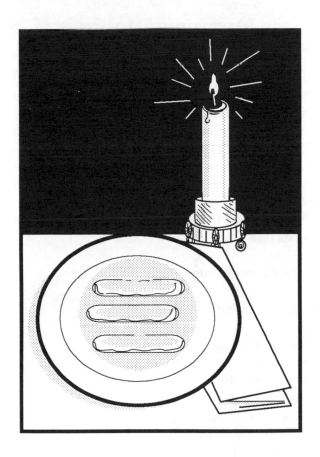

Mexican Diablo Crepe Crisps

Always alert for new ways to introduce tropical tastes into my kitchen, I brought the memory of this crepe dish back from the Caribbean coast of Mexico and re-created it. The original was served in a street corner cafe with so little pretense that they did not even put their name on the building. They advertised their cafe by the smell of the food.

Crepes (see page 90)

Diablo Crepe Filling
1/4 cup butter
1/4 cup chopped onions
1/4 cup flour
1/2 teaspoon mustard powder
2 teaspoons Pickapeppa Sauce
1/4 teaspoon salt
1/8 teaspoon ground turmeric
1/8 teaspoon ground cumin
2 tablespoons picante sauce
1 cup milk
1 cup (1/2 pound) crab meat

1 egg, beaten, divided
2 tablespoons milk
1 cup dried bread crumbs (about 3 slices), finely crushed
Oil to cover bottom of skillet about 1 inch deep

To make the filling, melt the butter in a heavy skillet over low heat. Increase the heat slightly and add the onions. Saute, stirring frequently, for 6 minutes.

Slowly add the flour, stirring constantly, to make a smooth roux. Cook, continuing to stir constantly, for 4 minutes.

Add the mustard, Pickapeppa Sauce, salt, turmeric, cumin, and picante sauce. Cook an additional 3 minutes, stirring occasionally. Add the milk and cook 4 to 5 minutes.

Blend the crab meat into the mixture. Continue to cook until the filling is thoroughly heated.

Keep the filling warm.

To assemble and finish the crepes, divide the filling mix into 12 equal portions. Set aside. Lay out the 12 crepes, with the attractive side of each crepe down.

Lightly beat the egg. Wash the inside edges of each crepe with egg to help hold the crepe together while cooking. Reserve the remaining portion of egg. Spoon 1 portion of the filling mix onto each crepe. Roll each crepe tightly and set aside.

Combine the reserved portion of the egg with the milk. Place the crushed bread crumbs nearby.

In a heavy skillet, heat the oil to medium high.

Coat each rolled crepe with the egg-milk mixture, then roll in the bread crumbs. When complete, fry each crepe in the oil a few at a time for 30 seconds to 1 minute each. Drain on absorbent paper. Serve hot.

Yield: 6 servings of 2 crepes each

Shari Clark's Crab Dumplings Étouffée

When these dumplings are boiled, they are magnificent with Shari's étouffée sauce. They also work very well with marinara or Alfredo sauce. I serve the fried dumplings with tartar or cocktail sauce.

1 1/2 cup (3/4 pound) **crab meat**
1/2 cup chopped **green onions**
1/2 cup chopped **green bell pepper**
1 tablespoon diced **pimento**
1/4 teaspoon **white pepper**
2 teaspoons prepared **mustard**
6 tablespoons **mayonnaise**
1 teaspoon **salt**
6 tablespoons **slivered almonds** (optional)
6 tablespoons **chopped celery** (optional)

36 **won ton wrappers**
1 **egg**, lightly beaten
Canola or **peanut oil** to fry, or **water** to boil

Étouffée Sauce for Boiled Dumplings
4 tablespoons **butter**
4 tablespoons **flour**
1 cup **chicken stock**
1/4 cup finely chopped **green bell pepper**
1/4 cup finely chopped **celery**
1/4 cup finely chopped **onion**
1/2 teaspoon **cayenne**
1/2 teaspoon **Tabasco**
1/2 teaspoon chopped **green bell pepper**
1 teaspoon **pepper blend** (see page 131)
1/2 cup (1/4 pound) **crab meat**

Combine the ingredients for the filling in a large mixing bowl.

To assemble the dumplings, set half the won ton wrappers aside to top each dumpling and lay out the other half of the wrappers for the bottoms. Brush each bottom wrapper with the lightly beaten egg. This will act as a sealer.

Spoon 1 1/2 tablespoons of the dumpling filling in the center of each bottom wrapper. Cover each bottom wrapper with the top wrapper. Using your fingers, press the top and bottom wrappers together around the filling mix.

Cut the dumplings out with a ravioli maker. If you do not have a ravioli maker, press a small drinking glass over each mound of covered filling and cut around the glass with a sharp knife. Leave about 1/4 inch of wrapper from the edge of the glass. Set the assembled dumplings aside to fry or boil.

To fry dumplings, heat the oil in a heavy skillet or pot at medium or at low-high. Fry each dumpling 30 seconds on each side until golden brown. Cook not more than 4 dumplings at a time. Drain on absorbent paper and serve.

To boil dumplings, bring water to a rolling boil. Drop each dumpling into the water, a few at a time. Boil them 5 minutes. Dumplings must be watched carefully: overcooked dumplings will come apart in the boiling water.

To make the étouffée sauce, make a roux of the butter and flour by slowly melting the butter in a heavy skillet. Add the flour slowly, stirring constantly. If lumps appear in the mixture, break them apart until the sauce is smooth. Continue to cook, stirring constantly, for 5 minutes.

Add the chicken stock in a thin stream, continuing to stir constantly. Stir in the bell pepper, celery, and onions. Add the cayenne, Tabasco, green bell pepper, pepper blend, and crab meat. Simmer for 15 minutes, stirring frequently. Serve hot.

Yield: 6 servings of 3 dumplings each

Crab Meat and Cheese Soufflé

One secret in cooking a soufflé in a modern oven is to be aware of the direction of heat. Ovens with strong top heating elements may cook the top of the soufflé so quickly that it crusts over and is prevented from rising. In this case you can move an oven rack to the lowest position before baking.

Bechamel Sauce
5 tablespoons butter
1/4 cup flour
1 cup milk

4 eggs, separated
1 cup grated cheddar cheese
1/8 teaspoon cayenne
1/8 teaspoon nutmeg
1 cup (1/2 pound) crab meat, patted dry

Prepare a soufflé dish by lightly oiling the sides and bottom with butter. After oiling, dust the oil coating with a thin coating of flour. With this preparation, the soufflé should cook without sticking to the sides and bottom of the dish. It is important to use a dish made especially for soufflés. The soufflé dish has straight sides that enable the soufflé to rise evenly.

To make the Bechamel sauce, melt the butter over medium heat until bubbly. Add the flour and cook about 1 minute, stirring constantly. Remove from heat, add milk, and whisk until smooth. Return to the heat and stir the egg yolks, cheese, cayenne, and nutmeg into the sauce. Stir continuously until the cheese has melted. Add the crab meat, heat and mix thoroughly. Set the mixture aside to cool.

Preheat the oven to 400 degrees F.

Prepare a clean glass bowl by washing it thoroughly with a teaspoon of vinegar. Dry the bowl completely. Add the egg whites and beat to firm peaks. If you continue to beat the egg whites after they have firmed, they will not combine well with the batter.

When the Bechamel mixture is cool, fold in the egg whites.

Bake in the prepared dish for 30 minutes or until firm and golden brown. Serve the soufflé immediately from the dish in which it was baked.

Yield: 6 servings

Crab Meat with Sherry Soufflé

Sherry is used in so many delicious dishes that it deserves at least one paragraph on its own. Sherry was first made in southeastern Spain during the Roman period. Centuries later when Spain began trading with England, barrels of this wine were shipped under the name Vino de Jerez, taking the name of the largest village of the area, Jerez de la Frontera. English shoppers liked the wine and anglicized its name to sherry. Sherry owes its unique taste to the addition of brandy during the wine-making process.

Bechamel Sauce (see page 94)

4 eggs, separated
1/2 cup sliced mushrooms
1/3 cup dry sherry
1/8 teaspoon ground nutmeg
1/8 teaspoon Tabasco
1/8 teaspoon pepper blend (see page 131)
1/4 teaspoon salt
1 teaspoon chopped fresh parsley
1 cup (1/2 pound) crab meat, patted dry

Prepare a soufflé dish by lightly oiling the sides and bottom with butter. After oiling, dust the oil coating with a thin coating of flour. With this preparation, the soufflé should cook without sticking to the sides and bottom of the dish. It is important to use a dish made especially for soufflés. The soufflé dish has straight sides that enable the soufflé to rise evenly.

To make the Bechamel sauce, melt the butter over medium heat until bubbly. Add the flour and cook about 1 minute, stirring constantly. Remove from heat, add milk, and whisk until smooth. Add the mushrooms and the sherry.

Return to the heat and stir in the egg yolks, nutmeg, Tabasco, pepper, salt, and parsley. Add the crab meat, heat and mix thoroughly. Set the mixture aside to cool.

Preheat the oven to 400 degrees F.

Prepare a clean glass bowl by washing it thoroughly with a teaspoon of vinegar. Dry the bowl completely. Add the egg whites and beat to firm peaks. Where you stop beating is crucial. If you continue to beat the egg whites after they have firmed, they will not combine well with the batter.

When the white sauce is cool, fold in the egg whites. Bake in the prepared dish for 30 minutes or until firm and golden brown. Serve the soufflé immediately from the dish in which it was baked.

Yield: 6 servings

Baked Crab Roll

While giving a lecture on cooking, I was once asked how cooks knew the temperature in their oven before they had thermometers, let alone before thermostats were invented. I was caught completely by surprise; the question had never crossed my mind. Later I researched oven temperatures and found that in the early days cooks often judged temperatures in wood or coal-burning ovens by the length of time they could hold their hand inside, much the same way many people today judge the heat on outdoor grills. Or they measured the time it took an oven to brown flour. Fortunately, we have better equipped ovens now. The only trouble you should have with this baked dish is curbing your appetite until it is done.

Stuffing

2 tablespoons butter
1/4 clove garlic, sliced
1 cup thinly sliced mushrooms
1 tablespoon soy sauce
1 teaspoon white wine vinegar
2 green onions, chopped
1 tablespoon chopped fresh parsley
2 tablespoons chopped fresh spinach
1/2 tablespoon prepared mustard
2 teaspoons Pickapeppa Sauce
1/4 teaspoon Tabasco
3 cups (1 1/2 pounds) crab meat
1 teaspoon lime juice
4 soda crackers, finely crushed
Milk to seal the pastry

Pastry

1 1/2 cups flour
1 teaspoon brown sugar
1/2 cup shortening
Ice water to bind

To prepare the stuffing, melt the butter in a large, heavy skillet over low heat. Add the sliced garlic, and saute 3 minutes, stirring frequently. Remove the garlic and discard. Add the mushrooms to the skillet. Saute 2 minutes, then sprinkle with the soy sauce. Stir to combine. Continuing to stir, saute the mushrooms for an additional 4 minutes.

Add the white wine vinegar, chopped green onions, parsley, and spinach. Continue to cook, stirring constantly, for an additional 4 minutes. Add more butter if all the oil is absorbed.

Stir in the mustard, Pickapeppa Sauce, and Tabasco.

Gently stir in the crab meat, taking care not to break any large pieces of crab. When the mixture is thoroughly heated, sprinkle the lime juice over all. Cook an additional minute, then remove from the heat.

Stir in the crushed soda crackers. Set the crab roll stuffing aside in a warm place.

Preheat the oven to 375 degrees F.

To make the pastry, sift the flour. Stir in the brown sugar. Cut in the shortening. Add the water and blend. On a floured surface, roll the prepared pastry into a 12x8x1/4 inch rectangle.

To assemble the crab roll, spoon the filling mix onto the center of the pastry. Wash the edges of the roll with milk. Pinch and seal at the top, and fold the sides of the crab roll in over one another.

Place the pastry in a lightly greased baking pan. Bake for 30 minutes. Remove from the heat and cut into individual portions and serve.

Yield: 8 servings

Old Fashioned Charleston Crab Meat Pie

This is an old family recipe given to me by Mrs. Brooks Peterson, a lady whose family lived in Charleston from the early 1800s until just after World War I. She said that in her grandparents' time vendors sold crabs door to door on a regular schedule very much like a milk route. Many of these vendors were the children or family of the fishermen, and it was not unusual to see the name of their father's vessel painted on the side of the basket or cart used to deliver the crabs.

1/4 cup butter
1 small green bell pepper, finely chopped
1 medium red onion, chopped
1/2 cup flour, sifted
1 teaspoon dry mustard
1 cup milk
1 tablespoon dry sherry
1 cup grated cheddar cheese
1 cup (1/2 pound) crab meat
1 No. 2 can tomatoes, drained
1 teaspoon Tabasco
1 teaspoon pepper blend (see page 131)
1/4 lemon
1 tablespoon chopped fresh parsley

2 teaspoons baking powder
1 cup flour, sifted
1/2 cup grated cheddar cheese
2 tablespoons butter, softened
1/2 cup milk

Melt the butter on low heat in a heavy skillet. Increase the heat; add the pepper and onion, and cook 8 minutes.

Stir in the flour, mustard, milk, sherry, and cheese, stirring constantly. Cook on low until the cheese is totally melted and the mixture has thickened. Stir in the crab meat, tomatoes, Tabasco, and pepper blend. Heat thoroughly.

Pour into a large casserole dish. Squeeze the lemon over the mixture. Sprinkle the top with the parsley. Set aside.

Preheat the oven to 450 degrees F.

To make the pastry topping, sift the baking powder with the flour. Mix in the cheese. Mash in the butter, then add the milk. Stir to combine. Spread in an even layer over the crab mixture.

Bake uncovered 20 minutes and serve.

Yield: 6 servings

Crab Ramekins

I make this when I want to serve a light lunch. If I have a leftover tablespoon of green bell pepper, chives, or shallots, I sometimes toss it in for good measure. Green salad is a good accompaniment.

Pastry
2/3 cup flour
1/4 teaspoon salt
3 tablespoons butter
1 tablespoon vegetable shortening
2 tablespoons cold water
1 egg white, beaten lightly

Filling
1/2 cup grated Parmesan cheese
1 cup (1/2 pound) crab meat
1/2 cup grated Swiss cheese
3/4 cup light cream
1 whole egg
1 egg yolk
1 teaspoon chopped fresh parsley
1/8 teaspoon nutmeg
1/4 teaspoon black pepper
1/4 teaspoon white pepper

Preheat the oven to 375 degrees F.

To make the pastry, sift the flour and salt together. Cut in the butter and shortening. Add the water and blend. Form the dough into a ball. On a floured surface, roll the dough out until it is about 1/8 inch thick. Line each ramekin loosely with the dough. Trim the excess from the edges of each ramekin. Bake the pastry for 5 minutes. Remove ramekins from the oven and brush with egg white. Set aside.

Raise the oven heat to 400 degrees F.

Divide the Parmesan cheese, crab meat, and grated Swiss cheese into 4 equal portions. Spread a layer of Parmesan, a layer of crab meat, and a layer of Swiss in each ramekin.

Gently heat the cream until it is warm. Combine the whole egg and the egg yolk. Lightly beat and stir into the cream. Add the parsley, nutmeg, and peppers, and stir to combine.

Pour the cream mixture into the ramekins, dividing equally.

Arrange the ramekins on a cookie sheet. Bake for 15 to 18 minutes and serve.

Yield: 4 servings

Artichokes Stuffed with Crab Meat

In the same spring months when crabs begin to reach the market is abundant supplies—March, April, and May—artichokes reach the peak of their flavor. Is it any wonder that they go so naturally together? The artichoke I used here is the globe artichoke, the most common variety in U.S. markets. Do not confuse with the globe artichoke, which is a tuber in the sunflower family and a different plant altogether.

4 artichokes
1 lemon slice

Stuffing Mix
1 tablespoon butter
1/4 cup olive oil
1/4 cup finely chopped celery
3 tablespoons finely chopped onion
2 teaspoons finely chopped garlic
1 1/2 cup (3/4 pound) crab meat
1 1/2 cups fresh bread crumbs (about 2 slices),
   crusts removed
1 teaspoon oregano
1 tablespoon thyme
1/2 teaspoon pepper blend (see page 131)
1/2 cup + 4 teaspoons chicken stock

To prepare the artichokes, first slice off the stem so that the artichoke sits upright. Use a sharp knife to remove the top inch of leaves from the artichoke cone. Rub the trimmed parts with the lemon; this part of the preparation is both for appearance and flavor. The trimmed parts will discolor if left untreated.

Next, cut off the sharp points of the rest of the leaves and remove any rough or inedible leaves from the base of the plant. Rinse the artichoke in cold water, gently working the leaves until they pull apart. Remove the purple leaves in the core of the artichoke. Scrape out the choke at the core of the plant. Rinse again, drain, and set the prepared artichokes aside on absorbent paper.

To prepare the stuffing mix, melt the butter in a saucepan. Add the olive oil. When hot, saute the celery, onion, and garlic stirring frequently. Cook until done, about 4 minutes. Stir in the crab meat, bread crumbs, and spices. Heat thoroughly.

Preheat the oven to 350 degrees F.

To prepare the dish, pour the 1/2 cup chicken stock in a baking dish. Stuff each artichoke with the stuffing mix, filling both the center and the surrounding leaves of the artichoke. If the artichoke does not seem to hold together firmly, you can tie it together with a string. Pour a teaspoon of the remaining chicken stock in the center of each artichoke. Cover and bake 30 minutes. Uncover and bake an additional 15 minutes. Serve immediately.

Yield: 4 servings

Crab with Asparagus

The flavor of this dish is better if you use fresh asparagus.

1/4 cup butter
1/4 cup flour
1 cup milk
1/2 cup dry white wine
2 cups (1 pound) crab meat
1 tablespoon chopped green bell pepper
1 teaspoon finely chopped shallots
2 teaspoons chopped fresh parsley
1 teaspoon Dijon mustard
1 teaspoon Pickapeppa Sauce
1 teaspoon lime juice
1 teaspoon pepper blend (see page 131)
1/2 teaspoon salt
1/8 teaspoon mace
2 eggs, lightly beaten
18 asparagus tips, canned or freshly cooked
1/4 cup grated Parmesan cheese

Using a heavy skillet, melt the butter over low heat. Increase the heat slightly and slowly add the flour, stirring constantly. Break up any lumps of flour to make a smooth sauce. Continuing to stir constantly, cook 5 minutes.

Add the milk and wine in thin streams. Stir to combine and cook until thick, about 4 minutes, stirring frequently.

Preheat the oven to 400 degrees F.

Add the crab meat and gently stir to combine. Add the remaining ingredients except the eggs, asparagus tips, and cheese. Stir gently and heat about 1 minute. Remove from the heat and stir in the eggs. Pour the crab meat mixture into a lightly greased baking pan. Arrange the asparagus tips in a layer over the crab meat, and top with the Parmesan cheese. Bake 25 minutes or until golden brown.

Yield: 6 servings

Canopy Garden Crab and Mushroom Casserole

Before my first visit to Manhattan my father told me, "If you don't look up, you'll miss it." He was right. But if you do more than look up—if you go up—there is even more to see, especially when the Big Apple puts on its evening dress. Perhaps somewhere a painter has the range to capture the colors and drama of New York after dark. I doubt it. I have never seen a painting, photograph, or video that did justice to New York's night cityscape. This crab meat and mushroom casserole is made at the Canopy Garden. The view there is worth sharing, and so is this crab dish.

2 tablespoons butter
1 cup thinly sliced mushrooms
1 tablespoon flour
1/2 cup light cream
2 cups (1 pound) crab meat
1/4 teaspoon curry powder
1 teaspoon chopped fresh parsley
2 egg whites, beaten
1/2 lime

Preheat the oven to 350 degrees F. Melt the butter in a heavy skillet over low heat. Add the mushrooms and saute for 5 minutes. Slowly add the flour, stirring constantly and cook for 3 minutes. Add the cream in a thin, steady stream. Simmer and stir until the mixture thickens, about 5 minutes. Add the crab meat, curry, parsley, and egg whites. Stir until thoroughly blended. Squeeze the lime juice over the mixture, and stir again. Cook on low for 2 minutes.

Pour the crab meat mixture into a greased dish and bake for 25 minutes.

Yield: 4 servings

Crab Meat with Broccoli

This dish is a sophisticated blend of flavors sparkled by the addition of lime zest. Zest is the peel of the lime just on the surface of the fruit. Its special flavor is contained in oil located in tiny sacs near the outer skin. In order to enjoy the full flavor of the oil, the sacs must be broken before adding the peel to the dish. This may be done by grating or rolling the lime on the counter pressing hard, before using a grater.

1 package frozen broccoli, cooked
2 cups (1 pound) crab meat
1 cup grated sharp cheddar cheese
1 cup sour cream
2 small tomatoes, very finely chopped, cooked
1 medium red onion, finely chopped
2 tablespoons lime juice
1 tablespoon lime zest
1 teaspoon prepared horseradish
1/2 teaspoon worcestershire
1/4 teaspoon dried thyme
1/2 teaspoon pepper blend (see page 131)
1/4 teaspoon garlic powder
1/4 teaspoon salt

Preheat the oven to 350 degrees F.

Lightly grease an oven-proof baking dish.

To prepare the casserole, arrange the broccoli in a greased baking dish. In a separate mixing bowl, combine the remaining ingredients. Stir gently until combined. Pour the crab meat mixture over the broccoli.

Bake the casserole 30 minutes and serve.

Yield: 4 servings

Crab and Cheese Stuffed Potatoes

Baked potato and cheese lovers will ask for this dish again and again. I like it especially on nippy, cool fall days when a hot potato satisfies the need for a warm place inside. An attractive yet simple presentation is to serve the stuffed potatoes on a bed of spinach or other green leaf.

4 medium baking potatoes
Butter or olive oil
2 cups (1 pound) crab meat
1 cup grated sharp cheddar cheese
1 tablespoon grated Parmesan cheese
1/2 cup butter
1/4 cup half-and-half
1/4 cup chopped green onions
1/4 teaspoon chopped fresh dill
1/4 teaspoon salt
1/4 teaspoon cayenne

Preheat the oven to 400 degrees F.

Select good, heavy baking potatoes. Wash the potatoes, then rub the skins with a light coating of softened butter or olive oil. Bake the potatoes for 1 hour, or until done.

Remove the potatoes from the heat and allow them to become cool to the touch. Cut the potatoes lengthways. Scoop out the cooked potato pulp from the inside, being sure to leave the potato skins intact. Reserve the potato pulp.

Raise the heat to 425 degrees F.

Place the potato pulp in a large mixing bowl. Add the remaining ingredients. Stir this mixture until it is thoroughly mixed.

Divide the stuffing mix into 8 equal portions. Stuff one portion of the mix into each potato skin. Arrange the potato skins in a lightly greased, shallow oven-proof baking dish.

Bake for 15 to 20 minutes and serve.

Yield: 8 servings

Marilyn Van Zandt's Crab-Stuffed Mushrooms

I named this dish for Marilyn Van Zandt, the only person I have ever known who kept a crab as a pet. The crab, a land crab named Oscar, was a Florida native. Marilyn kept it in the house and fed it bacon. Marilyn told me that she had the crab trained to click its claws and beg for food. Crab story or not, at least this recipe is not a put on. Serve it and watch your guests click their forks begging for more.

1 pound large mushrooms
1 tablespoon softened butter
4 tablespoons butter, divided
1/4 cup finely chopped shallot
1 cup (1/2 pound) crab meat
1/4 cup sour cream
1 egg, lightly beaten
2 cups soft bread crumbs
1 tablespoon chopped fresh parsley
1 teaspoon soy sauce
1/2 teaspoon pepper blend (see page 131)

Wash the mushrooms carefully. Divide the stems from the caps. Very finely chop enough of the stems to make 1 cup. Set aside.

Thinly coat the mushroom caps with the softened butter. Set aside.

In a heavy skillet, melt 2 tablespoons of the butter on low heat. Add the chopped mushroom stems and the shallots. Increase the heat slightly and saute for 3 minutes. Remove from the heat.

Add the crab meat, sour cream, egg, 1/2 of the bread crumbs, parsley, soy sauce, and pepper blend to the sauteed mushrooms and shallots. Gently stir until thoroughly combined.

Preheat the oven to 375 degrees F.

Arrange the mushroom caps cap down in a shallow, greased oven-proof baking dish. Spoon the crab meat mixture into the mushroom caps.

In a separate pan, slowly melt the last 2 tablespoons of butter. Toss with the remaining cup of bread crumbs Sprinkle this mixture over the mushroom caps. Bake for 15 minutes and serve.

Yield: 4 servings of 4 or 5 caps each, depending on size of mushrooms

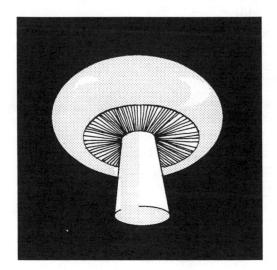

Stuffed Bell Peppers

This dish uses a thick, finely flavored Creole sauce to add relish to the taste and aroma of crab-stuffed bell peppers. Creole cooking is often indentified with hot peppers, but classic Creole cooking is really not defined by pepper or heat. Creole cooking uses as a base the country French method common to the early French settlers of Louisiana. To this was added the later influence of Spanish, African, West Indian, and English settlers, as well as the influence of the original Indian inhabitants. It is a combination of adapted ingredients and evolved techniques, a truly American cuisine.

Creole Sauce

2/3 cup canned tomatoes
1 tablespoon olive oil
1 tablespoon chopped fresh basil
1/2 clove garlic, very finely chopped
1/4 teaspoon pepper blend (see page 131)
1/8 teaspoon Tabasco

1 cup (1/2 pound) crab meat
2 cups cooked rice
1/4 cup finely chopped celery, including tops
2 eggs, lightly beaten
1/4 cup butter
4 green bell peppers, cleaned and seeded

Prepare the sauce by combining the ingredients. Simmer over low heat for 20 minutes, stirring frequently. Set aside, but keep warm.

Preheat the oven to 375 degrees F.

Make a stuffing mix by combining the crab meat, cooked rice, celery, and eggs. Stir gently but thoroughly, and divide into 4 equal portions.

In a separate pan, melt the butter slowly over low heat. Stuff each pepper with 1 portion of the stuffing mix. Pour the melted butter over the stuffed peppers, dividing equally.

Select a small enough baking pan that the peppers can be arranged for baking without tipping over. Add about 1 inch of water to the pan.

Bake the peppers for 10 minutes. Remove from the oven and baste the tops of the peppers with creole sauce, about 2 tablespoons per pepper. Return to the oven and bake an additional 20 minutes.

Serve immediately.

Yield: 4 servings

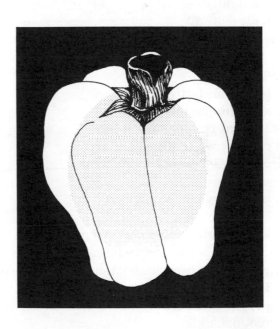

Crab Meat Omelet

In this delicately flavored omelet, shallots lend just a touch of spicy snap. Shallots are members of the onion family, but with a flavor somewhere between a mild onion and garlic. When buying shallots at market, select bulbs in the same way you would garlic. They should have a dry, slightly brittle skin and should be firm and free of spots. Avoid bulbs that have begun to sprout. If you are not able to obtain shallots, substitute one teaspoon of very mild onion, and lightly rub the inside of your mixing bowl with a freshly cut garlic.

Omelet Mixture
8 eggs, lightly beaten
1/2 teaspoon salt
1 teaspoon pepper blend (see page 131)

Filling
2 tablespoons butter
2 teaspoons chopped shallots
2 teaspoons chopped fresh basil
1/4 cup dry white wine
1 1/2 cups (3/4 pound) crab meat

4 tablespoons butter, divided

It is important when making an omelet to start with eggs at room temperature. If the eggs are refrigerated, set them out about an hour before using.

To make the omelet mixture, stir the eggs, salt, and pepper blend briskly with a fork for about 30 seconds. Set aside.

To prepare the omelet filling, heat 2 tablespoon of butter in a skillet. Saute the shallots 2 minutes, then add the basil and wine and cook on low heat for an additional 3 minutes, stirring constantly. Add the crab meat, toss to combine, and heat thoroughly.

Divide the filling into 4 portions. Set aside in a heated oven.

Cook one omelet at a time. Heat the skillet or omelet pan over medium heat with 1 tablespoon butter. Tilt the pan in a circular motion to cover the bottom and sides of the pan with butter. Pour on 1/4 of the omelet mixture. Repeat the circular motion of the pan to set the egg evenly. Stir the top of the uncooked omelet mixture rapidly with a fork while shaking the pan back and forth to help the eggs cook evenly. When the omelet is done, probably a minute or less, spoon 1 portion of the filling onto half of the omelet. Fold the other half of the omelet over the half containing the filling. Remove to a heated plate. Repeat these instructions for each omelet.

Yield: 4 servings of 1 omelet each

Blue Crab Omelet

Blue crab meat is the ideal mate for the gentle flavor of eggs and cheese. This omelet is simple to make and a real pleasure to eat. I serve this at breakfast with a fruit cup. For lunch or supper I accompany the omelet with roughly sliced fried potatoes.

Filling Mixture
2 cups (1 pound) crab meat
2 cups half-and-half
2 tablespoons sliced green onion
1/2 teaspoon dried thyme
1/2 teaspoon salt
6 drops Tabasco
2 tablespoons flour
1/4 cup water

Omelet
12 eggs
1 1/2 teaspoons salt
1/8 teaspoon black pepper

1/4 cup margarine, divided
1 1/2 cups grated cheddar cheese, divided

Make sure the eggs are at room temperature. If the eggs are refrigerated, set them out about an hour before using.

To make the filling mix, combine the crab meat, half-and-half, onion, thyme, salt, and Tabasco. Heat thoroughly over medium low heat. Blend the flour and water together and add to the filling mix. Cook until thick, stirring constantly.

To make the omelets, beat together the eggs, salt, and pepper. Cook one omelet at a time. Heat 2 teaspoons margarine in an omelet pan until the margarine sizzles. It should not be so hot as to burn the margarine.

Pour 1/6 of the omelet mixture into the omelet pan. Cook on low until the omelet is almost done. Sprinkle 1/4 cup cheese on top and continue to cook until the cheese melts.

To complete the omelet, place 1/2 cup of the crab meat mixture on one half of the omelet. Fold the other half of the omelet over the filled half.

Repeat this procedure with each omelet. Serve hot.

Yield: 6 servings of 1 omelet each

Crab Frittata

This is a Tidewater delicacy, from the area beginning roughly on Maryland's eastern shore and extending south through Virginia. I have seen variations of this recipe which go back to colonial times when a splendid style of entertaining was enjoyed in the big plantation houses of the region. With cotton and tobacco valuable trade items, European commerce was important to the economies of the southern states bordering the Atlantic. In common with many of the dishes that evolved there, this recipe has hints of French cuisine.

2 tablespoons butter
1 1/2 cups (3/4 pound) lump crab meat
3 small potatoes, boiled and finely cubed
2 eggs, lightly beaten
2 tablespoons chopped red bell pepper
1 tablespoon finely chopped shallots
1/2 teaspoon salt
1/8 teaspoon curry powder
1 teaspoon chopped fresh parsley
1/2 teaspoon pepper blend (page 131)

In a heavy skillet, melt the butter over low heat.

In a mixing bowl, combine the remaining ingredients. Add to the skillet and cook over medium heat, stirring constantly, for 4 minutes.

Reduce the heat to very low. If all of the oil has been absorbed in the first part of the cooking process, add a bit more to moisten the bottom of the skillet.

Using a flat utensil, press the ingredients in the skillet to make a flat, cake-like disk.

Cover, and cook for an additional 6 minutes without stirring or turning the cake. When done, tip the skillet over to turn out the cake.

Serve immediately, with the attractive, skillet side up.

Yield: 4 servings

Crab Meat with Scrambled Eggs

For full flavor, crab meat should be used as soon after cooking as reasonably possible. This tasty breakfast is an excellent use for crab meat left over from the day before. It is a meal in itself, or delicious served with hash browns.

4 eggs, lightly beaten to a uniform color
4 strips bacon (ham or sausage can be substituted)
2 tablespoons finely chopped onion
1/2 teaspoon salt
1/2 teaspoon pepper blend (see page 131)
3/4 cup (3/8 pound) crab meat
1/4 teaspoon curry powder

Start with the eggs at room temperature. If the eggs are refrigerated, set them out about an hour before using.

Chop the bacon into small bits and fry until almost done.

Add the onion, and cook until tender, about 3 minutes.

Add the eggs, salt, and pepper. Scramble the eggs and cook until they are firm, stirring and turning frequently.

Stir in the crab meat and curry powder. Combine thoroughly and heat.

Yield: 4 servings

Crab Quiche

Serving a quiche is like wearing a tuxedo—always in style. This easy-to-prepare quiche can be served as a main course or as an appetizer with equal success. I think that it makes a great lunch served with a simple green salad or a cup of fruit.

1 cup flour
1/4 teaspoon salt
1/4 cup butter
1 1/2 tablespoons vegetable shortening
3 tablespoons cold water

3 eggs
1 cup light cream
1/2 teaspoon salt
1 teaspoon lemon juice
1/8 teaspoon white pepper
1/4 teaspoon nutmeg
1 1/2 cups (3/4 pound) crab meat
1/4 pound grated Swiss cheese
2 tablespoons butter

To make the pie crust, preheat the oven to 375 degrees F. Sift the flour and salt together. Cut in the butter and shortening. Add the water and blend. Form the dough into a ball. On a floured surface, roll the dough out until it is about 1/8 inch thick and forms a circle about 12 inches across. Place the dough loosely in a 9-inch pie pan. Trim the excess from the edges of the pan. Bake the pie crust for 5 minutes. Remove from the oven and set aside.

To prepare the quiche mixture, beat the eggs lightly. Add the cream and beat again. Stir in the salt, lemon juice, pepper, and nutmeg.

Reduce oven heat to 350 degrees F.

Spoon the crab meat into the prepared pie crust. Cover the crab meat with the grated Swiss cheese. Pour the cream mixture over the cheese, and dot with bits of butter.

Place the uncooked quiche on a cookie sheet. Bake for 45 minutes. Serve warm.

Yield: 6 servings

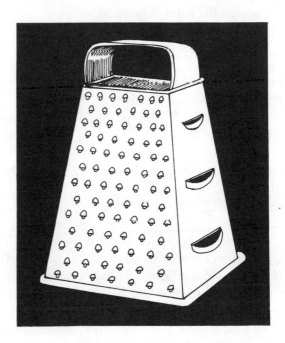

Crab Croquettes

Crab croquettes are a favorite of mine. This recipe was give to me by Ann Harding Bonneau of Mobile, Alabama. It is a very old southern recipe. Harding family tradition attributes it to the family of Jefferson Davis, the president of the Confederate States of America.

2 tablespoons butter
2 tablespoons flour
1/3 cup chopped red onion
2 cloves garlic, finely chopped
1 tablespoon chopped fresh parsley
1 tablespoon very finely chopped celery
1 cup milk
2 tablespoons heavy cream
2 cups (1 pound) crab meat
2 tablespoons finely chopped bell green peppers
1/3 teaspoon salt
1/2 teaspoon black pepper
2 cups bread crumbs (about 6 slices, altogether),
  divided
2 eggs, lightly beaten, divided

Using a heavy skillet, make a roux by melting the butter over low heat. Increase the heat slightly and slowly add the flour, stirring constantly. Break up any lumps of flour to make a smooth paste. Continuing to stir constantly, cook 5 minutes.

Add the onions, garlic, parsley, and celery, and stir to combine. Cook an additional 5 minutes. Add the milk and cream in a thin, steady stream. Let simmer very slowly for 3 minutes.

Add half the beaten eggs and 1 cup bread crumbs to the remaining ingredients. Mix thoroughly and form the mixture into inch-thick patties.

Dip each patty first into the remaining egg, then dredge with the remaining crushed bread crumbs. Saute in just enough butter to cover the bottom of a skillet. Cook on medium low low heat until each side is thoroughly browned. Drain on absorbent paper and serve.

Yield: 4 servings

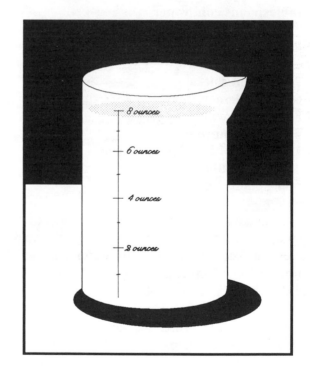

Rice, Mushroom, and Crab Meat Croquettes

This mixture of flavors and textures is sure to please the most demanding palate. I serve this with simple steamed vegetables and a green salad lightly dressed with vinegar and oil. Garlic toast brushed lightly with olive oil is a good accompaniment.

2 tablespoons butter
1/3 clove garlic, sliced
1 cup sliced mushrooms
2 tablespoons soy sauce
1/4 teaspoon black pepper

1/2 cup butter
1/4 cup flour
1 cup milk
1 teaspoon prepared mustard
1/8 teaspoon cumin
1/8 teaspoon turmeric
2 cup (1 pound) crab meat
1 cup cooked rice
1/4 lemon

To prepare the mushrooms, melt 2 tablespoons butter in a large, heavy skillet over low heat. Add the sliced garlic and saute 3 minutes, stirring frequently. Remove the garlic and discard. Add the mushrooms to the skillet. Saute 2 minutes, then sprinkle with the soy sauce. Stir to combine. Continue to stir and cook the mushrooms. Add the pepper, and cook an additional 4 minutes. Remove to a warm oven and reserve.

Using a small saucepan, melt the butter over low heat. Keep warm enough to remain a liquid.

Make a roux. Heat 1/4 cup of the melted butter on low heat in a small pan. Add the flour slowly, stirring constantly. The mixture should be smooth and free of lumps. Break apart any lumps that form while you are blending. Continuing to stir, cook the roux for 4 minutes on low heat.

Add the milk, mustard, cumin, and turmeric to the roux. Blend thoroughly. Simmer an additional 5 minutes.

Preheat the oven to 400 degrees F.

Add the crab meat and sauteed mushrooms to the roux. Blend and allow to heat thoroughly, then combine with the cooked rice. Remove the croquette mixture from the heat.

Divide the croquette mixture into either 4 or 8 equal parts, depending on the size croquette desired. Shape each portion into a croquette patty.

Squeeze the lemon into the remaining 1/4 cup melted butter.

Arrange the croquettes on a lightly greased baking pan. Brush the croquettes liberally with the lemon butter.

Bake for 15 minutes. Remove the croquettes from the oven and baste liberally once more with the lemon butter. Immediately turn the croquettes, baste again, and return to bake for another 15 minutes.

Yield: 6 servings

Hot Crab Sandwich— Open Faced

Cheese lovers are sure to like this open-faced crab sandwich. It is so simple to make, it practically puts itself together. To give the sandwich a special kick, I use the sharpest cheddar I can buy. My favorite side dishes are premium potato chips and cole slaw.

6 English muffins, split
1/4 cup butter
1 cup grated Swiss cheese
1 cup grated sharp cheddar cheese
2 cups (1 pound) crab meat
Paprika to dust

Preheat the broiler to 550 degrees F. Arrange the split muffins, split side up, on a cookie sheet.

To make the sandwich spread, melt the butter in a heavy skillet over low heat. Stir both of the cheeses into the butter and stir until the cheese is totally melted.

Fold the crab meat into the cheese mixture and immediately spread the combination on the muffin halves. Dust the sandwiches with paprika.

Broil the hot sandwiches until they are golden brown, about 2 minutes, and serve.

Yield: 6 servings

Baked Crab Sandwich

This sandwich is good with store-bought bread, but if you make your own loaf, it is even better. Compared to what our ancestors went through to make bread, baking bread today is easy. In the first half of the nineteenth century, two necessary ingredients for bread, baking powder (1856) and yeast cakes (1868), were not even sold in stores. Homemade baking powder was compounded from cream of tartar, bicarbonate soda, and either flour or cornstarch. Yeast was made from hops or potatoes and had to be started almost a week ahead. Charitably put, results were mixed. A cook with a reputation for reliable baking powder and yeast was a community treasure. Today we have overcome the difficulties of earlier ages and you will get more predictable results.

1 loaf French bread

1/3 cup sour cream
1/3 cup mayonnaise
1 cup (1/2 pound) crab meat
1/3 cup grated sharp cheddar cheese
2 tablespoons finely chopped tomatoes
2 tablespoons finely chopped onions
1/4 teaspoon garlic powder
1 tablespoon lemon juice

Slice the loaf of French bread lengthways. Pull out enough bread from inside the loaf to make room for the filling. Set aside.

Preheat the oven to 375 degrees F.

To make the stuffing, place the mayonnaise and sour cream in a mixing bowl. Stir to combine. Add the crab meat, cheese, tomatoes, onions, and garlic powder and thoroughly blend. Sprinkle the lemon juice over the mixture and stir.

Stuff the crab meat mixture into the cavity in the French bread. Place the bread in an aluminum foil "boat," open at the top. Bake for 25 minutes. Remove from the oven and slice into 4 to 6 equal portions, depending on serving size desired, and serve.

Yield: 4 to 6 servings

Crab and Shrimp Baked Casserole

Nothing is better than crab except shrimp and nothing is better than shrimp except crab. For me to cook crab and shrimp in the same dish is a little like going to a party and having two lovers show up—I just don't know what to say. But you'll know what to say after you have prepared this baked casserole—magnificent!

1 pound uncooked shrimp, shelled and deveined
3 cups water
4 teaspoons salt

1 cup mayonnaise
2 tablespoons olive oil, if using bottled mayonnaise
1 cup (1/2 pound) crab meat
1 cup finely chopped green bell pepper
1 cup finely chopped celery
1/4 cup finely chopped red onion
2 teaspoons Pickapeppa Sauce
1/2 teaspoon pepper blend (see page 131)
1/4 teaspoon salt
1 tablespoon butter
1/2 clove finely minced garlic
1 cup dried bread crumbs (about 3 slices)

Bring the water to a rolling boil and add the salt. Add the shelled and deveined shrimp and cook for 4 to 5 minutes, depending on the size of the shrimp. Drain, rinse with cool water, and set aside.

If you are using bottled mayonnaise, place the mayonnaise in a glass or stainless steel mixing bowl. Add the olive oil in a fine stream, stirring constantly. Continue to stir until the oil is thoroughly blended into the mayonnaise. Set aside.

Preheat the oven to 350 degrees F.

To make the casserole, combine the boiled shrimp, mayonnaise, crab meat, green pepper, celery, onions, Pickapeppa Sauce, pepper blend, and salt in a large mixing bowl. Stir until well blended.

Pour the crab meat mixture into a lightly greased, oven-proof baking dish or into ramekins.

In a separate saucepan, melt the butter over low heat. Saute the garlic for 3 minutes, then toss the garlic butter with the dried bread crumbs. Sprinkle the garlic bread crumbs over the casserole.

Bake for 30 minutes and serve.

Yield: 8 servings

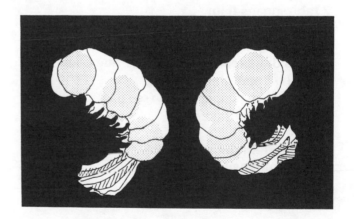

Flounder with Crab Meat Stuffing

For a seafood lover, fine texture and well-defined flavor mark crab meat as a natural stuffing ingredient. This recipe has an interesting blend of flavors to compliment the flounder and tickle your palate. I serve this when I really want to put on a show. I like to serve it with green salad, a sauced vegetable, and a lightly toasted garlic bread.

Stuffing

2 tablespoons butter
1 clove garlic, finely chopped
1 teaspoon finely chopped shallots
2 tablespoons flour
1/4 cup heavy cream
1/2 cup dry white wine
3 slices dry bread, crushed into fine crumbs
1 cup (1/2 pound) crab meat
1/2 teaspoon pepper blend (see page 131)
1 lime, juice of

1 pound flounder (4 fillets)
1/4 cup softened butter
1 lime, juice of
1 slice dry bread, crushed into fine crumbs

To prepare the stuffing for the flounder, melt the butter in a heavy skillet over low heat. Add the garlic and shallots, and saute, stirring frequently, for 4 minutes.

Slowly add the flour, stirring constantly, and cook for an additional 4 minutes.

Pour in the cream in a thin stream, stir, and cook 1 minute, but do not allow to boil. Blend the wine to the mixture. Add the bread crumbs, crab meat, pepper blend, and lime juice to the skillet. Stir until thoroughly combined. Set aside to cool.

Preheat the oven to 350 degrees F.

To make the stuffed flounder, divide the stuffing mix into 4 equal portions. Heap 1 portion of the stuffing mix onto each flounder fillet. Shape each stuffed fillet into a roll. Tie the fillets with string if necessary.

Arrange the stuffed fillets in a lightly buttered baking dish. Spread each flounder roll with an equal portion of the softened butter. Sprinkle with the lime juice and the bread crumbs. Bake 30 minutes and serve.

Yield: 4 servings

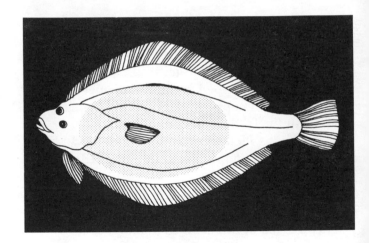

The Anchorage Crab-Stuffed Rainbow Trout

John Gilbertson shared this recipe with me while he was executive chef of the Anchorage in Houston, Texas. The Anchorage is one of Houston's premier restaurants offering seafood in a unique environment. The walls are built from the teak deck planking of the USS Astoria. The S.S. Exton and the S.S. Matar, two early freighters, furnished the buffets. Ship wheels, barometers, compasses, binnacles, ship bells, and other nautical artifacts are exhibited. The nautical decorations are not reproductions; they are real, like the food.

I enjoyed this meal with Linda Haskins. Chef Gilbertson served us this dish accompanied with a rice pilaf and sauteed mushroom caps. Chef Gilbertson is now with American Airlines.

1 cup (1/2 pound) crab meat
1/4 pound bread crumbs
1/2 bunch green onions, whites only, chopped
1 lemon, juice of (about 3 tablespoons)
1 egg
1/3 cup heavy cream
1/4 teaspoon salt
1/4 teaspoon white pepper

1/2 pound butter
1 tablespoon lemon juice
1/4 cup white wine

4 rainbow trout, cleaned and boned

To prepare the crab meat stuffing, combine the crab meat, bread crumbs, green onions, and lemon juice. In a separate bowl, combine the egg and the heavy cream. Add the crab meat mixture to the egg mixture and stir. Season with salt and pepper to taste.

Transfer to a double boiler and cook over medium heat for 45 minutes, stirring frequently.

To prepare the lemon butter, clarify the butter by slowly melting the butter in a saucepan. Remove from the heat and allow the oil and the sediments to separate. Drain away the clear, clarified butter from the top of the mixture. Return to low heat. Stir in the lemon juice and set aside.

Preheat the oven to 350 degrees F.

To assemble the dish, arrange the cleaned, boned trout in a baking pan. Fill the cavity of each trout with an equal portion of the stuffing mix, about 4 ounces. Baste liberally with the lemon butter and the white wine. Keep the wine separate from the lemon butter.

Bake the stuffed trout for 9 to 12 minutes, until the fish flakes easily. Serve immediately with the remaining lemon butter as a dipping sauce.

Yield: 4 servings

John Clancy's Crab Meat Stuffed Coho Salmon

This dish is served in John Clancy's, in the heart of New York's Greenwich Village. The recipe for this excellent entree was brought to my attention by C.P. McIlhenny of the McIlhenny Company, makers of Tabasco sauce. Mr McIlhenny kindly arranged for John Clancy's permission to share his recipe for this book.

Stuffing
1 1/2 cup (3/4 pound) crab meat
1/2 cup mayonnaise
1/4 cup chopped scallions
3 tablespoons finely chopped red pepper
3/4 teaspoon Tabasco
1/2 teaspoon salt

4 Coho salmon, cleaned and boned
2/3 cup flour
12 ounces clarified butter or olive oil

Lemon Pine Nut Sauce
2 cups chicken stock
2 tablespoons lemon juice
1 teaspoon Tabasco
8 ounces cream cheese
4 ounces pine nuts, toasted
1 tablespoon chopped fresh parsley

Preheat the oven to 450 degrees F.

Combine the crab meat, mayonnaise, scallions, red pepper, Tabasco, and salt. Fill the cavity of each fish with 1/2 cup of the stuffing.

Flour both sides of each stuffed fish.

Unless you have a skillet large enough to hold more than 1 fish at a time, you will have to prepare each fish separately and hold it in a warmed oven until the rest are done. To prepare a fish, heat 3 tablespoons of clarified butter or olive oil. Brown the fish on each side until golden, about 3 to 4 minutes per side. Place the fish in the oven for 10 minutes, turning the fish once.

Prepare the Lemon Pine Nut Sauce by bringing the stock to a boil. Add lemon juice and Tabasco and return to a boil. Add the cream cheese in pieces, whisking constantly. Reduce mixture until slightly thickened, about 3 minutes. Add the nuts and parsley, then salt to taste.

Serve immediately, with the sauce on or alongside the fish.

Yield: 4 servings

Crab Salads, Cold and Hot

Crab Louis

Legends, so often the only source of information on the origin of famous recipes, credit Crab Louis to the chef of the Olympic Club in Seattle, Washington. The classic Crab Louis is made with Dungeness crab, although other varieties of crab meat are often used. Like so many famous dishes, crab louis has no definitive recipe. I hope you enjoy my version.

3/4 head iceberg lettuce, shredded
3 cups (1 1/2 pounds) lump crab meat
1 lime
4 tablespoons chili sauce
1/2 cup mayonnaise
1 teaspoon olive oil
1 teaspoon chopped capers
1 teaspoon finely chopped fresh chervil
1 tablespoon very finely chopped green bell pepper
1 tablespoon very finely chopped green onion
Paprika

Lettuce leaves
2 teaspoons olive oil
1 teaspoon vinegar
1/8 teaspoon salt
1/4 teaspoon black pepper

Place the shredded lettuce in a large bowl. Sprinkle the crab over the top of the lettuce, then squeeze the lime over the crab meat.

Combine the chili sauce, mayonnaise, and 1 teaspoon olive oil. Stir until thoroughly blended, then stir in the capers, chervil, green peppers, and green onions.

Toss the chili sauce mixture with the lettuce and crab meat mixture. Toss carefully so that the lumps of crab meat will not be broken to pieces.

Dust the salad with paprika. Set aside to chill.

In a separate bowl combine the olive oil, vinegar, salt, and pepper. Stir to mix. Lightly coat the lettuce leaves with the vinegar and oil mixture and arrange the leaves on serving plates.

To serve the Crab Louis, spoon the crab meat mixture onto the beds of lettuce arranged on the serving plates. Serve slightly chilled.

Yield: 6 servings

Hanalei Bay Crab Salad

This Hawaiian salad is a rich, flavorful treat that makes an excellent light lunch. I like to serve it outdoors without dressing—it really doesn't need any. A glass of dry white wine sets this salad off marvelously.

1 1/2 cups (3/4 pound) lump crab meat
1/3 cup freshly grated coconut meat
1/2 teaspoon coriander
2 teaspoons finely chopped shallots
1 tablespoon lemon juice
2 papayas, halved and stoned
Salad greens, lettuce or spinach

Mix the crab meat, coconut, coriander, and shallots in a large bowl. Do not stir so vigorously that the delicate lump crab meat is broken into pieces. Lightly sprinkle the lemon juice over the crab meat mixture.

Assemble the salad by placing the cleaned papaya halves on the salad greens. Spoon the crab meat mixture into the cavities of the papaya halves.

Yield: 4 servings

Louisiana Crab Salad

Every spring I look forward to the first days when I can eat outdoors. That is the time of year when I go through my recipe file and take out my best salad and summer dishes and begin making up a list of people to share them with. Each year this is one of the recipes I pull out. I serve it with lightly buttered garlic toast on the side. I hope that you enjoy this dish as much as I do.

3 cups (1 1/2 pound) lump crab meat
3/4 cup peanut oil
1/2 cup white wine vinegar
1/4 cup parsley
3 whole green onions, chopped
1 tablespoon paprika
2 teaspoons prepared horseradish
1 teaspoon dry mustard
1 teaspoon Tabasco
1/2 teaspoon mace
1 1/2 cups shredded lettuce
1 1/2 cups shredded spinach
Salad greens, lettuce or spinach

Combine all of the ingredients except the shredded lettuce, shredded spinach, and the salad greens. Stir the mixture until the ingredients are thoroughly combined. Do not stir so vigorously that the fragile lumps of crab meat are broken. Set the mixture aside to chill.

In a large bowl, combine the shredded lettuce and shredded spinach. Toss with the crab meat mixture until blended, again being careful not to break the crab meat apart.

Assemble the salad by arranging a bed of salad greens on serving plates. Spoon the crab meat salad mixture on the greens. Serve slightly chilled.

Yield: 8 servings

Tangy Crab Salad

The pleasures of summer always seem more sharply defined while seated at an outdoor table with a seafood feast before me. Pleasant company makes such an occasion even better. This is one of the foods I enjoy when eating an outdoor lunch. The spices have just a bit of tang. Cool fruits and wine are my favorite accompaniments.

2 cups (1 pound) lump crab meat
1/2 cup ketchup
1/4 cup finely chopped green bell peppers
3 tablespoons prepared horseradish
2 tablespoons lime juice
2 teaspoons Dijon mustard
1/4 teaspoon curry powder
1/4 teaspoon black pepper

Lettuce leaves
2 teaspoons olive oil
1 teaspoon vinegar
1/8 teaspoon salt
1/4 teaspoon black pepper

Combine the lump crab meat, ketchup, green peppers, prepared horseradish, lime juice, mustard, curry powder, and 1/4 teaspoon ground black pepper. Gently stir the ingredients, taking care not to break the delicate pieces of lump meat apart. Set aside.

In a separate bowl combine the olive oil, vinegar, salt, and pepper. Stir to mix. Lightly coat the lettuce leaves with this mixture and arrange the leaves on serving plates.

Spoon the salad on the bed of coated lettuce leaves and serve.

Yield: 4 servings

Chilled Crab Meat and Avocado Salad

This salad is a little upscale, guaranteed never to bore your guests. When I want to do something extra, I marinate ripe tomatoes at room temperature in balsamic vinaigrette and serve them as wedges on the side. At other times I serve orange or apple wedges.

2 tablespoons olive oil
1 tablespoon tarragon vinegar
1 teaspoon lime juice
1 1/2 cups (3/4 pound) lump crab meat
1/3 cup chopped celery
1 teaspoon capers, drained and chopped
1 tablespoon chives
2 avocados, halved and stoned
Salad greens, lettuce or spinach

Dressing
1/2 cup mayonnaise
1 tablespoon olive oil
1 tablespoon finely chopped red bell pepper
2 teaspoons chopped fresh parsley
1/2 teaspoon celery seeds
1/2 teaspoon finely chopped red onion
1/4 teaspoon white pepper
1/8 teaspoon salt

In a glass or steel bowl, beat the olive oil, vinegar, and lime juice together. Add the crab meat, celery, capers, and chives. Stir gently to mix, being careful not to break apart the fragile pieces of crab lump meat. Cover the salad and set aside to chill.

In a separate bowl, prepare the dressing. Add the olive oil to the mayonnaise and stir until they combine. Add the rest of the dressing ingredients and blend thoroughly. Set aside to chill.

Assemble the salad by placing the avocado halves on the salad greens. Fill the avocados with the crab meat mixture. Spoon the dressing over the stuffed avocado halves and serve.

Yield: 4 servings

Crab Slaw

I re-created this recipe from a dish I was served while visiting Historic River Street in Savannah, Georgia. In earlier times when Savannah was a busy shipping point, River Street was the heart of Savannah's commercial district. Large sections of the city near the water's edge have since been renovated and are now filled with shops, restaurants, and interesting places. On pleasant afternoons, River Street takes on the aspect of an outdoor party.

1 cup shredded red cabbage
2 cups shredded green cabbage
1/2 cup thinly sliced green bell peppers
1 stalk celery, chopped, including leaves
1 small onion, sliced into thin half rings
3 cups (1 1/2 pounds) lump crab meat

1/4 cup mayonnaise
1/4 cup olive oil
1/4 cup white wine vinegar
1/2 teaspoon garlic powder
1 teaspoon dry mustard
1/2 teaspoon salt
1/2 teaspoon pepper blend (see page 131)
1/4 teaspoon Tabasco

In a large mixing bowl, combine the red and green cabbage, green pepper, celery, onion, and crab meat. Stir together gently. Set the mixture aside.

In a separate bowl, prepare the dressing by combining the mayonnaise and olive oil. Add the vinegar and stir. Blend in the remaining ingredients.

To make the crab meat slaw, pour the dressing over the vegetable and crab meat mixture. Move the ingredients around in the bowl until the vegetables are lightly coated with the dressing. Serve slightly chilled.

Yield: 8 servings

Crab Slaw with Dill

A hint of dill sets off the flavor of other spices as well as providing a flavor of its own. When using dill, it is important to know if the recipe calls for dill seed or dill weed, both of which come from the same plant. Of the two, the weed is more delicately flavored. If you grow your own dill, harvest the dill weed when the plant is blooming for peak flavor.

1 cup finely shredded cabbage
1/2 cup sliced mushrooms
1/2 cup finely chopped celery
1 tablespoon finely chopped shallots
1 1/2 cups (3/4 pound) lump crab meat

6 tablespoons salad oil
2 tablespoons white wine vinegar
1/2 cup finely grated cucumber
1/8 teaspoon dry mustard
1/8 teaspoon pepper blend (see page 131)
2 teaspoons honey
1 tablespoon finely chopped fresh dill weed

In a large mixing bowl, combine the shredded cabbage, mushrooms, celery, shallots, and crab meat. Stir together, but do not stir so vigorously that the tender pieces of lump crab meat are broken apart. Set the mixture aside.

In a separate bowl, prepare the cucumber and dill dressing. Combine the oil and vinegar. Add the remaining ingredients and blend thoroughly. Set the dressing aside to chill.

To assemble the salad, toss the cabbage and crab meat mixture carefully together with the dressing. Serve immediately, slightly chilled.

Yield: 4 servings

Baked Crab Meat and Avocado Delight

Southwestern cuisine offers so many choices it is hard to know where to turn first. This baked crab meat and avocado salad is equally good as a main or a first course. The smooth, buttery flavor of avocado is the perfect counterpoint to salad's peppery spiciness. I serve corn chips and Mexican relish on the side.

2 cups (1 pound) lump crab meat
1/4 cup sweet pickle relish
1/4 cup mayonnaise
1/4 teaspoon salt
1/4 teaspoon pepper blend (see page 131)
1/8 teaspoon cayenne
1/8 teaspoon Tabasco
3 avocados, halved and stoned
1/2 cup grated Monterey jack cheese

Preheat the oven to 375 degrees F.

Mix the crab meat, pickle relish, mayonnaise, salt, pepper blend, cayenne, and Tabasco.

Arrange the avocado halves, cut side up, in a shallow baking dish. Divide the crab meat stuffing equally and fill each avocado with the mixture. Sprinkle the grated cheese over the prepared avocados. Bake 30 minutes and serve.

Yield: 6 servings

Sauces
for Dipping
and Marinating

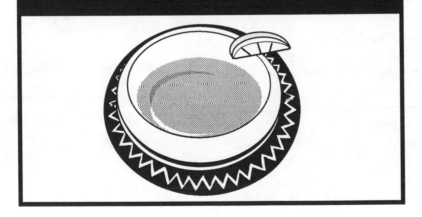

Crab Butter

Use crab butter when making delicately flavored sauces, especially for seafood. It is good when brushed on toast or crackers used as a base for appetizers, and it is a superb basting or dipping sauce for fish.

Basic Recipe
shells from 4 blue crabs or 2 Dungeness crabs
1 cup butter
1/2 cup water

Garlic Crab Butter
1 clove garlic, sliced in quarters

Lemon or Lime Crab Butter
1/4 lemon or 1/2 lime

Crab Butter with Parsley
2 tablespoons chopped fresh parsley

For the basic crab butter recipe, preheat the oven to 200 degrees F. Arrange the crab shells on a cookie sheet or aluminum foil. Place the crabs shells in the oven, and allow to dry for 20 minutes.

Wrap the shells in a clean, heavy cloth, then beat with a mallet until the shells have been reduced to fine crumbs. Set aside.

Melt 1 cup of butter over low heat. Add the crushed shells and 1/2 cup warm water. Simmer the mixture 15 minutes. Do not allow the butter to become so hot that it burns.

Remove from the heat and strain the mixture. Set aside in the refrigerator until the butter has cooled. When the mixture has cooled, remove the butter from the top of the water. This is your crab butter.

For garlic crab butter, place 1 tablespoon of the crab butter in the pan, and slowly melt it over low heat. Add the garlic, increase the heat, and saute the garlic 4 minutes. Discard the garlic. Add the remaining butter and reduce the heat to low.

For lemon or lime crab butter, squeeze the juice from the citrus fruit into the melted crab butter a few minutes before the butter is removed from the heat.

For crab butter with parsley, simply sprinkle the parsley into the crab butter immediately after straining. Gently stir to combine.

Yield: about 1 cup of crab butter

Herb Dipping Sauce for Crab Meat

Use the best quality mayonnaise and the freshest herbs for this sauce. I recommend making your own mayonnaise. In addition to a dipping sauce, this also makes a flavorful spread for crab cake sandwiches.

1 cup mayonnaise
2 tablespoons olive oil, if using bottled mayonnaise
1/4 cup finely shredded spinach leaves
1/4 cup finely chopped fresh parsley
1 teaspoon lime juice
2 tablespoon finely chopped fresh chives
1/4 teaspoon salt
1/4 teaspoon white pepper

If you are using bottled mayonnaise, place the mayonnaise in a glass or stainless steel mixing bowl. Add the olive oil in a fine stream, and stir until the oil is thoroughly blended into the mayonnaise. Add the remaining ingredients. Mix well and chill.

Yield: about 1 1/2 cups of sauce

Mustard Dipping Sauce

There are many fine mustard dipping sauces. This one uses one of my favorite flavors, dill. Make this as you would the other recipes in this book calling for mayonnaise, preferrably with homemade mayonnaise. Fresh dill leaf will add flavor that dried leaves will lack. As does Herb Dipping Sauce, this serves as an excellent spread for crab cake sandwiches.

1 tablespoon dry mustard
1 tablespoon water
3/4 cup mayonnaise
1 1/2 tablespoons olive oil, if using bottled mayonnaise
1/4 cup finely chopped fresh dill weed
1/4 teaspoon salt
1/4 teaspoon pepper blend (see page 131)

To prepare the mustard sauce, mix the dry mustard with the water, and stir until thoroughly combined.

If you are using bottled mayonnaise, place the mayonnaise in a separate bowl. Add the olive oil in a fine stream, stirring constantly. Continue to stir until the oil is thoroughly blended into the mayonnaise.

Add the mayonnaise to the mustard. Stir in the remaining ingredients. Mix thoroughly, and set aside to chill.

Yield: slightly more than 1 cup of sauce

South Florida Mustard Dipping Sauce

This finely seasoned dipping sauce for crab claws is especially appropriate for the delicious, meaty claws of the stone crab. Deanna Ryan, a lifelong resident of the Florida keys gave me this recipe over the telephone. After Ms. Ryan listed the ingredients, I asked her how she put them together. These are her instructions: "Now, honey, you want to make your own mayonnaise, that's important. If you can't do that, use some olive oil and beat it up good. Now you know about worcestershire. You can use a little less if you want to. Put in everything else. Keep stirring it up. Use more Tabasco if you want to or put in some other pepper. Some people do this with lemon, but if you don't put in some kind of juice it won't be right. The little limes we have down here are the best but you probably can't get them there."

1 cup mayonnaise
2 tablespoons olive oil, if using bottled mayonnaise
1 tablespoon dry mustard
1 tablespoon worcestershire
1/4 teaspoon Tabasco
1/4 teaspoon salt
1/2 teaspoon lime juice

If you are using bottled mayonnaise, place the mayonnaise in a glass or stainless steel mixing bowl. Add the olive oil in a fine stream, stirring constantly. Continue to stir until the oil is thoroughly blended into the mayonnaise.

Add the rest of the ingredients and stir until well combined. Set aside to chill.

Yield: slightly more than one cup of sauce

Tropical Zest Chilled Sauce

This is a versatile sauce, useful as a dipping sauce as well as a sauce for crab cakes. I have also used it as a dressing for salads. Citrus zests are the key ingredients here, but to achieve the full tropical tang from the zests, it is essential that they be grated.

1 cup mayonnaise
1 teaspoon lime juice
1 teaspoon lemon juice
2 teaspoon tangerine juice
Grated zest from 1 lime
Grated zest from 1 lemon

Combine the ingredients and gently stir until thoroughly blended. Keep refrigerated and serve chilled.

Yield: 1 cup

Red Dipping Sauce

This is a red sauce that does not burn your tongue and kill your taste buds the way some of the hotter red sauces do. Serve it on the side or heap crab meat onto a bed of lettuce and spoon this sauce in the center. Sometimes I toss crab meat in this sauce until the meat is lightly coated, then spoon the dressed crab meat onto lettuce. Any way that you serve this sauce, it is good.

3/8 cup mayonnaise
2 teaspoons olive oil, if using bottled mayonnaise
3/8 cup ketchup
3/8 cup sour cream
1/8 teaspoon cayenne
2 teaspoon Pickapeppa Sauce
2 teaspoons dill pickle relish
2 teaspoons chopped fresh parsley

If you are using bottled mayonnaise, place the mayonnaise in a glass or stainless steel mixing bowl. Add the olive oil in a fine stream, stirring constantly. Continue to stir until the oil is thoroughly blended into the mayonnaise.

Add the rest of the ingredients and stir to combine. Set aside to chill.

Yield: slightly more than 1 cup of sauce

Red Devil Dipping Sauce

People with a taste for the tang of horseradish and pepper will relish this dipping sauce. Serve with crab claws or spooned over heaping mounds of crab meat on a bed of lettuce. Crackers and cool white wine compliment the flavor of this sauce.

1 cup bottled ketchup
2 teaspoons worcestershire
2 teaspoons prepared horseradish
2 teaspoons lime juice
1 teaspoon salt
1 teaspoon white pepper
1 teaspoon black pepper
1/2 teaspoon garlic powder
1/2 teaspoon onion powder

Combine the ingredients in a mixing bowl. Stir until thoroughly combined. Chill at least an hour before serving.

Yield: slightly more than 1 cup of sauce

Kathy Shaw's Crab Claw Marinade

My friend Kathy Shaw studied cooking at the Trianon Palace Hotel in Versailles and at the Cordon Bleu and Prue Leith cooking schools in London. This recipe is one of her secrets for giving crab meat salads the extra something that lifts them above ordinary. Before preparing the salad, marinate the crab for 30 minutes in this marinade. Kathy told me that one of the keys to this marinade is imported Parmesan cheese.

1/4 cup olive oil
1/4 cup canola oil
1/4 cup tarragon vinegar
1 cube white sugar
1 teaspoon Dijon mustard
1/2 teaspoon salt
1/2 teaspoon black pepper
1/2 teaspoon prepared horseradish
1 tablespoon grated Parmesan cheese

Mix the 2 oils. Set aside.

Reserving the cheese, combine the remaining ingredients in a blender. Blend on slow speed. Then slowly add the oil in a continuous stream to make an emulsion. After the emulsion is made, slowly stir in the cheese.

Gently rinse the crab claws to remove any loose pieces of shell. Place the crab claws in a shallow bowl or dish.

Pour the marinade over the crab claws. Cover and allow to marinate at least 3 hours. Drain and serve. Use the drained marinade as a dipping sauce.

Yield: enough for at least a dozen crab claws

Base for Red Sauces

With this recipe you can have fully flavored red sauces without having to spend precious hours each time you make one. The secret is to make a base, simmer it for hours until the flavors are fully released, and then store it away to be used as the primary ingredient of another sauce you will make later.

4 green bell peppers, seeded and finely chopped
12 tomatoes, finely chopped
1 large red onion, finely chopped
1 cup cider vinegar
1/3 cup white sugar
2 teaspoons cinnamon
1/2 teaspoon cloves
1/2 teaspoon salt

Combine the ingredients. Simmer for 1 hour, stirring occasionally. Run through a blender for consistency. Return to the heat. Simmer for an additional 2 hours, continuing to stir occasionally.

Pour into prepared canning jars. Stored in the refrigerator, the sauce base will keep almost indefinitely.

When you are ready to make the sauce you will bring to your table, simply saute whatever you want to add that day to make the sauce special. You may cook garlic, celery, green bell pepper, or some other fresh vegetables. You can add additional spices, including pepper, if you want to add heat. You may even add cooked seafood—shrimp, crab meat, or finely chopped fish. With this flavorful base you cooked days or weeks before as a shortcut, in only a few minutes, you can serve a sauce that tastes as if cooked all day.

Yield: about 5 cups

Base for Mayonnaise Sauces

The simplest dressing for crab meat is a good, homemade mayonnaise. When accompanied by a plate of lemon wedges and a loaf of crusty French bread there is no finer presentation. Mayonnaise takes about 30 minutes to make. The quality, taste, and fragrance is superior to even the best commercial products.

2 egg yolks
1 teaspoon prepared mustard
1/4 teaspoon salt
1/4 teaspoon cayenne
1/4 teaspoon paprika
2 cups olive oil
2 tablespoons lime juice

All of the ingredients should be at room temperature before you begin. Beat the egg yolks until they are thick. Add the mustard, salt, cayenne, and paprika and continue to beat until the ingredients have thoroughly combined.

Add the oil, a drop at a time, beating slowly but continuously. After half of the oil has been used, gradually increase the flow of the oil until all of the oil has been added. If the flavor of olive oil is too strong for your taste, substitute peanut oil. Beat the lime juice into the mixture, then chill well. If you prefer the flavor of lemon you can use it, but use only half as much juice.

Mayonnaise is subject to spoiling—it absolutely must be refrigerated after preparation.

Yield: about 1 pint

Creole Sauce for Crab Cakes

Surely the most agreeable way to see friends is across the table. Something about food polishes wit and refines virtue. And what company wouldn't feel witty and refined while dining on crab cakes set off by this rich Creole sauce. Served hot or cold, this sauce is sure to become as much a favorite of yours as it is mine. Spoon the sauce lightly over crab cakes or serve in a gravy boat.

1 tablespoon canola or peanut oil
3 tablespoons chopped onion
3 tablespoons chopped green bell pepper
3/4 cup canned tomatoes, with juice
1 tablespoon chopped pimento
2 teaspoons white sugar
1/4 teaspoon salt
1/8 teaspoon pepper blend (see page 131)
1/8 teaspoon Tabasco

Heat the oil in a heavy skillet over medium low heat. Add the chopped onion and green pepper and saute until tender, about 5 minutes. Add the remaining ingredients, stir to combine, and simmer until thickened, about 20 minutes. Stir frequently. This sauce can be refrigerated and reheated, or served immediately. Spoon generously over crab cakes.

Yield: slightly more than 1 cup of sauce

Mustard Sauce for Crab Cakes

Piping hot crab cakes sometimes call for an equally hot sauce. I re-created this sauce from one I was served at a country inn on the Virginia side of the Potomac River. I was seated overlooking the water. Outside was the first cold wind of the winter and it came with a blustery force that shook the window in its frame. Rain was blowing in sheets across the river by the time the menu came. The server recommended the crab cakes and when I found that the sauce was heated, I asked for it. While we ate, my companion and I amused ourselves by guessing the ingredients.

2 tablespoons butter
2 tablespoons flour
1 cup milk
1/3 cup chicken broth
2 tablespoons Dijon mustard
1 tablespoon Pickapeppa Sauce
1 teaspoon finely chopped shallots
1/8 teaspoon pepper blend (see page 131)

Make a roux. Using a heavy skillet, slowly melt the butter over low heat. Add in the flour a little at a time, stirring constantly so that the mixture remains smooth. Increase the heat slightly, and cook over medium low for 4 minutes, stirring constantly.

Remove from the heat. Stir in the milk and chicken broth. Return the mixture to the heat, reduce to low, and simmer until thickened, about 45 minutes.

Add the mustard, Pickapeppa Sauce, shallots, and pepper blend. Spoon the hot sauce over the crab meat.

Yield: slightly more than 1 cup of sauce

Tomato Cognac Sauce for Crab Cakes

Finishing touches are all important. The quality of the cognac and the freshness of the herbs are all important in this sauce. In is also important not to shorten the simmering time. During this slow process, the full flavors of the ingredients are released. If you want to cook ahead, the sauce can be chilled and reheated immediately before serving.

2 tablespoons olive oil
1 ounces butter
1/2 large onion, finely chopped
1/4 garlic clove, very finely chopped
1/2 can tomato paste
1 1/2 cups tomato juice
1/2 teaspoon dried thyme
1/2 teaspoon dried sage
1 teaspoon dried marjoram
1/8 teaspoon salt
1/8 teaspoon pepper blend (see page 131)
2 tablespoons cognac

In a heavy skillet, melt the butter over low heat. Add the olive oil, and shake the skillet to combine. Add the onion and saute 2 minutes, stirring frequently. Add the garlic and continue to saute and stir. Cook on low an additional 5 minutes.

Reserving the cognac, add the remaining ingredients. Simmer covered for 1 hour over very low heat, stirring occasionally.

Add the cognac. Stir to combine. Cook an additional 3 minutes.

Spoon this hot sauce over the crab cakes.

Yield: slightly more than 1 cup of sauce

Crab Boil and Other Seasonings

When I think of crabs and the wide variety of spices used to enhance the delicate flavor of this wonderful little shellfish, I can not help returning in my mind to a lunch of steamed crabs I enjoyed several summers ago. The restaurant was well known and had built its reputation on its service of steamed and boiled crabs, plainly cooked and plainly served. The setting was perfect, a terrace overlooking the ocean. The sky was a gorgeous robin's egg blue and the pleasant conversation was accompanied by the calling of sea birds as they swooped and turned over the triangular sails of small pleasure boats filled with weekend sailors.

The proprietor was inordinately proud of his recipe for the spices he poured over the crabs as they cooked. He happily presented me with a large container of the spice but would not reveal the spices in the blend. Over and over he stated that when people came to his restaurant they often licked the spices from the shells of the crabs after eating the crab meat, and he felt that such a secret was too dear to share.

Actually, he did not need to bother. The distinctive spice he shook liberally over his crabs was composed predominantly of rough salt, with a bit of cayenne added for heat, and a pinch of garlic powder thrown in for good measure. He had made a good, easily prepared spice befitting a commercial kitchen, but the finger-licking dedication displayed by some of his customers was no more complicated than the tendency some people have to drown everything they eat in salt.

Many spice blends claiming to be flavor magicians are merely salt tricked up with a bit of this and that and poured into colorful containers suitable for grocery shelves. Do not be deceived; the central business of seasoning is taste, and taste is more than salt. The primary challenge faced by a cook approaching the spice rack is to bring out subtleties of flavor, especially when preparing a delicately flavored dish such as crab.

Sadly, some people have even come to equate heat with spice, and seek dishes so highly peppered that the taste of the food is little more than a vehicle providing texture for taste-killing heat. Curiously, the sources often named for these dishes, Mexico and Spain, do not smother the flavor of their food with heat. Indeed, some of the most subtly flavored dishes in the world are from these two countries. Spain, in particular, offers food to satisfy the most demanding gourmet.

Crab Boil

Surely the most basic spice in preparing crabs is a good crab boil. Crab boil, like the five-spice and curry powders from the East, is not a single spice, but a blend of other spices. There are as many recipes for this as there are crab cooks, and it would be difficult to find a spice more subject to interpretation and personal taste. Many dedicated crab cooks have their own crab boil, often made from a recipe honored by both years and ancestral approval.

I like this crab boil. It is simply made from readily available ingredients and makes a delicate and flavorful addition to boiled or steamed crabs. Store the crab boil in a tightly sealed jar away from direct sunlight. It should keep for at least a year. As the crab boil nears the end of its life, let it steep longer in the boiling water before adding the crabs in order to achieve full flavor.

Simply combine the ingredients. This recipe should make about 1/2 cup of crab boil.

5 whole cloves	2 teaspoons salt
5 bay leaves, crumbled	1/4 teaspoon allspice
1 teaspoon celery seed	1/2 teaspoon mace
3 tablespoons mustard seed	
1/2 teaspoon cayenne pepper	
1/2 teaspoon onion powder	
1/4 teaspoon garlic powder	
3 tablespoons black peppercorns	

If you want to buy crab boil already blended, Zatarain's Crab Boil (New Orleans, Louisiana) and Old Bay Seasoning (Baltimore Spice Company, Baltimore, Maryland) are good choices. Both are readily available at larger stores. Tabasco brand crab boil is available by mail order (800-634-9599).

Pepper Blend

In many of the recipes in this book you will find pepper blend listed as an ingredient. This is a favored spice for me, one I developed to add interest and complexity to a meal while avoiding the temptation to add pepper at the expense of flavor.

Pepper blend is a mixture of black, white, and cayenne (red) pepper. Before blending these peppers, you should freshly grind the black and white peppers from peppercorns. All kitchen stores sell special grinders for this purpose. The importance of freshly ground pepper can not be overstated. Whole peppercorns, if properly stored, will retain full flavor almost indefinitely. Once ground, however, the full flavor of the pepper declines rapidly and is significantly diminished after only a few months on the shelf. Cayenne, usually purchased already ground, is produced by a different plant from black and white pepper and is not as subject to flavor loss.

To make pepper blend, combine 2 parts freshly ground black pepper, 2 parts freshly ground white pepper, and 1 part cayenne. After mixing, store out of direct sunlight. In my own kitchen, I use this blend instead of the plain ground black pepper favored in most kitchens.

The reason I take the trouble to blend peppers is that each of the three peppers I mix has a different taste, reacts on the tongue at a different time while eating, and leaves a different aftertaste. I find the result more interesting, more satisfying than the simpler taste of a single pepper.

From time to time I am asked about pink peppercorns. In the last few years pink peppercorns have become a common item in specialty markets. This spice is about the size and shape of more familiar black, white, and green peppercorns but has a somewhat reddish color, from which it takes its name, and a somewhat bitter taste.

The plant that produces pink peppercorns is not related to the plants from which we obtain black, white, green, or cayenne peppers. Pink peppercorns are native to Brazil, where they grow on the Schinus terebinthifolius tree, which is related to poison ivy.

Many years ago, pink peppercorn trees were planted by French traders on Reunion Island in the Indian Ocean. The plants thrived, and now Reunion is our principal source of the spice. Most of the harvest is processed in France.

Trees bearing pink peppercorns have also been introduced into Florida and Hawaii where they now grow wild. In the southern United States, this tree is usually called Brazilian Pepper Tree or Florida Holly. The blooming season is November and December.

Like poison ivy, pink peppercorns are slightly toxic. Although I know that many people enjoy spicing their foods with this colorful little berry, I do not use it, nor do I recommend it.

Other Spices

Not all useful spices are colorful powders or leaves stored carefully away in spice racks. Some of the most flavorful spices are liquids. I suppose that a purist would say, perhaps accurately, that these are not spices at all but condiments. I would not argue the question at length, but when I use something as a spice, why should I not call it a spice?

One of my favorite liquid ingredients is Tabasco sauce, made since 1868 by the McIlhenny family of Avery Island, Louisiana. Tabasco sauce is a liquid pepper sauce made from a unique recipe that provides a heated but flavorful addition to seafood and other recipes. The McIlhennys maintain quality by growing their own peppers. They also blend and age the sauce themselves. There are a number of pepper sauces on the market that are similar to Tabasco. Some of these are quite good, but I favor Tabasco brand and it is the pepper sauce I have specified as an ingredient in many of the recipes in this book. All large grocery stores carry it. If you have never tried Tabasco sauce, you should.

Another liquid spice that is a regular in my kitchen is Pickapeppa Sauce. I discovered this tangy little treat while vacationing in Jamaica. To my surprise, I found that it was marketed in the United States but had not arrived in my little corner of the world. At present I am happy to say, Pickapeppa Sauce is available at larger grocery stores almost everywhere. If you can not find it in your area, write to the importer, Warbac Sales Company, P.O. Box 9279, Metairie, LA, 70055, for a source near you. This sauce has been made since 1921 by the Joseph Lyn Kee Chow and Tenny Cha-Fong families of Shooters Hill, Jamaica, and is certainly worth trying. In recipes calling for Pickapeppa Sauce you can substitute worcestershire sauce, but the taste will not be the same.

When creating your own crab recipes or personalizing an existing recipe, it is useful to know the herbs and spices that bring out the best in crabs. This is not a complete list, and the herbs and spices listed do not all go well with one another, but this list will give you a starting point. You will achieve better, more flavorful results with fresh herbs than with dried. After you have experimented a bit, you or your family will probably add other spices to my list:

basil	fennel	nutmeg
bay leaves	garlic	paprika
black pepper	green bell pepper	parsley
caraway	mace	rosemary
chives	marjoram	tarragon
curry	mustard powder	thyme

If you do decide to create your own recipes, do not forget that the foundation of your dish is the crab meat, and that your dish will succeed or fail on the taste of the crab. Let the crab be the star, and the seasonings supporting actors. Allow each to play its part but do not allow the delicate meat of the crab be overwhelmed by spices. Begin experimenting by adding less than you think you need of a given spice and call for comments afterward. As you become more experienced, become more bold.

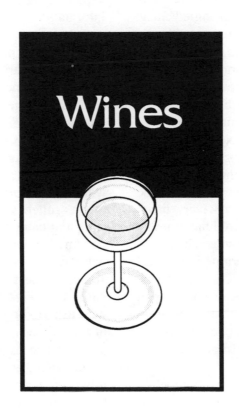

Wines

Wine complements crab both during cooking and later at the table. While this book is not a wine guide, some things will be useful for you to know while planning a crab meal. If you are truly knowledgeable about wine, you can skip this section entirely. I write here for the novice, whose confusion I personally recall.

If you are just learning about wine, I encourage you. You are on the brink of learning the zest that wine can add to a meal, both as an ingredient in cooking and later at the table. A properly selected wine can make a good meal a superb one. It can also save a marginal entree. The appropriate wine adds flavor and elegance to a meal. But how can you learn what to use, what to try? All the bottles look the same, and the labels do not offer much help.

I started drinking wine with meals before I had any sort of commitment to learn about wine or, for that matter, before I knew that there really was anything to learn. I found the foreign words on the labels intimidating, so I didn't think very much about what the labels might have told me. I developed a straightforward approach to wine selection— I tried a little of everything and returned to those I enjoyed.

My untutored start may have been a blessing in disguise. Simply buying the wines that I think taste good has proved a valuable touchstone, helping me again and again, leading me away from pretentious mistakes and fads.

Still, it is true that I made quite a number of purchases that I did not choose to repeat. Maybe with more help I would have learned more and enjoyed my selections more fully. There are several things you can do to help yourself. The first and probably the most important suggestion is to buy from a wine shop that enjoys a good reputation among wine connoisseurs. Inevitably, a store of this type will have someone on staff who is knowledgeable and willing to share information. Seek this person out. It

may or may not be the person at the counter. Ask for advice. A wine professional will not only be acquainted with what is on hand in his or her store but may be able to introduce you to wine periodicals on sale in the shop that may give you additional help.

I recommend buying a good wine book. While considering purchasing a wine book, do not be seduced by one of the large coffee table books rich with beautiful pictures. You are buying this book for information, not to decorate your living room. A useful wine guide should present specific information for a large number of wines from various countries and for various years. You really need a wine guide at the wine racks in the local wine store, not at home. Therefore, the book should fit easily into your pocket or purse.

A perfect example of a useful wine guide is *Hugh Johnson's Encyclopedia of Wine* (Simon & Schuster, Inc., New York). This slender little volume is packed with useful information. It is published annually and is an excellent guide for a novice. Any good bookstore will have it in stock or available for order.

Any business as competitive as the wine trade will have fairly well defined norms for the quality you can expect within any given price range. The purpose of wine education is not to discover a $75 wine in a $15 bottle; it will not happen. The purpose of a wine education is get the best wine to serve your needs and tastes at whatever price you wish to pay. All else being equal, a person who is knowledgeable is likely to walk out with a better wine for the money than a person who simply takes whatever comes to hand.

Do not fall into the trap of thinking that French wines are necessarily better than domestic or other European bottles. While it is still true that the best wines carry French labels, a French label does not guarantee the best wine. Many domestic wines are truly excellent and the better wines from Germany, Italy, and Spain are very good indeed. With the exchange rate as it is today, the better California and New York State wines may prove your best value.

If you are on a budget (as most of us are), remember that there are lots of tasty, affordable wines that are excellent choices, and the more you educate yourself, the more likely you are to find them.

If you are just starting out, once you have found some wines you like, put away a few bottles of each. Unless you are planning to keep them for a very long time, you don't need an elaborate wine cellar or expensive rack to keep them. Any place that is reasonably cool where you can lay the bottles on their sides will do. My first wine cellar was a closet floor.

Keeping a few bottles that you know you like on hand will make it easier to experiment. If you find that your next purchase is not to your taste, you can use it for cooking and bring out the tried-and-true.

Cooking with wine is easy. It is not the least bit difficult to learn.

I cook with the same wine I am drinking. Adding a bit to what I am cooking seldom lowers the bottle by much, and I have found that a wine that goes with the table usually goes with the pot.

I think of wine as an addition to my spice rack. Like spices, a little goes a long way. What you are seeking is a hint of flavor, not a taste that overpowers the other ingredients.

If you are trying a recipe that does not call for wine as an ingredient, you have an opportunity to experiment. Recipes are not chemical formulas, including the ones in this book. Change my recipes, add to them, substitute and experiment. You may find that the flavor has been changed (dare I say improved?) in a way that is more to your taste than the original.

Wine should be added early in the cooking process to give the alcohol time to evaporate from the dish. Wine adds a subtle flavor to foods. You should give this flavor time to mingle with the other flavors released in your food during cooking.

Wine added too late during cooking will retain calories which otherwise would have evaporated away. In addition, raw alcohol left in the dish may leave a harsh taste that can detract from delicately flavored dishes such as crab.

The use of wine as a seasoning has a special benefit for people who want to cut back on the sodium in their food. The acids and natural salts in wine are quite close to the chemical composition of table salt and stimulate the same taste buds. A bit of wine added to a dish can help satisfy the craving for salt that almost all of us have.

Some people use cooking wines. I do not. Cooking wine is really just cheap wine with salt added. The practice originated in an earlier time in commercial kitchens. Inn keepers opened wine for the chef to use while cooking. Adding salt to these bottles was a means of keeping the wine in the pot rather than having it disappear into the cook. Knowing this, it is easy to see why you do not need it in your kitchen. If you habitually serve wines too dear to be used at the stove, simply buy an inexpensive bottle of something compatible. Even the least expensive sale-of-the-week wine will be an improvement over cooking wines.

On the following page are some appropriate wines to consider for crab and crab dishes. If in doubt, remember that most good dry whites will work quite nicely with most crab dishes. If your meal is crab meat dipped in lemon or lime butter, try one of the lighter wines. If you are serving a crab dish with a robust sauce or heavy seasoning, try one of the more full-bodied wines.

Medium to Full-Bodied Wines	Medium to Light Wines	
Chardonnay	Chablis	Mosel
Meursault	Champagne	Muscadet
White Bordeaux	Chenin Blanc	Pinot Blanc
White Burgundy	Gavi	Riesling
	Liebfraumilch	Sauvignon Blanc

For a final word on wine, I will share with you one last bit of advice: avoid the wine snob. By wine snob I do not mean a person who likes fine wines and is curious enough to enlarge his or her appreciation by study; a person like this can be a wealth of information as you learn and develop your own taste. To me a wine snob is someone who goes out of the way to make people feel that they can not possibly know enough to enjoy what they are drinking.

Really, I suppose I am talking about a wine bully. Who knows how many people have given up furthering their knowledge of wines because it was made to seem a hopelessly difficult task? Rubbish. Remember my cardinal rule for wine selection: drink what you enjoy with whatever you enjoy drinking it with. You don't have to do a scientific analysis or learn to read French to watch your guests and see what they enjoy.

Most important of all, approach wines with a spirit (no pun intended) of adventure and a readiness to learn. In no time you will discover what is right for your table.

Glossary

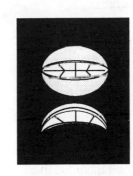

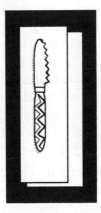

From the 4,400+ species of crabs, I have described the ones you are most likely to encounter in North American markets. From other parts of the world I included only the crabs you are most likely to hear about from well-traveled Americans or find specified in a foreign recipe.

Some of the "crabs" described in the glossary are not crabs at all but other creatures, often unrelated to crabs, many of which are not even edible. While I was passing this manuscript around my circle of friends for comment several asked me why I included these "crabs" with the true crabs.

The reason is simple: If enough people say that a thing is a crab, a crab it shall be, though a thousand Ph.Ds dissent. People have a mania for naming (usually after themselves) everything that walks, crawls, swims, or flies. Occasional flashes of logic appear in this naming process, such as when a creature is being christened with its scientific name. But who other than a scientist uses scientific names?

Another question raised was why I included in a cookbook glossary species of crabs that are almost never eaten, even when present in large numbers, such as species of crabs measuring less than an inch after achieving full growth. I had two reasons for placing crabs from this group in this glossary. First, just because a species of crab is seldom eaten does not mean that it is never eaten. Second, this information may save someone, hearing that a particular crab is plentiful, from expecting to make a meal from it.

In this glossary, I tried to include as many colloquial and slang expressions for crabs as possible, but I have been around fishermen too much to think that this is the full measure of their creativity in the language arts. I have aimed for the more common words that somehow have not made it into ordinary dictionaries. I hope that you find it useful.

Alaska king crab: See king crab.

Alaska snow crab: See spider crab.

American mussel crab: See oyster crab.

apron: The removable back shell underneath the crab; also the tail. Narrower on the male than the female, which uses the extra width to protect her eggs. The apron is also called the "T" or the tab.

Atlantic snow crab: See spider crab.

ballie: A female crab carrying roe, or eggs.

bay crab: Used to refer to the smaller specimens of Dungeness crabs. This term entered the language because the Dungeness crabs taken from bays and estuaries were observed to be smaller than crabs caught in the open sea.

berry: The roe, or eggs, of the female crab.

berry or berried crab: A female crab carrying roe, or eggs.

big crab: See rock crab.

birgus crab: See robber crab.

black crab: See land crab.

black-fingered crab (Lophopanopeus heathii): This is a small crab inhabiting United States Pacific coastal waters. It seldom grows larger than an inch and has no commercial value. The color of the shell varies from white to red, but the tips of the claws are always black.

blue crab (Callinectes sapidus): The scientific name for the blue crab must have been selected by someone who was partly a poet and partly a gourmet. Calli is Greek for beautiful, and nectes is Greek for swimmer. The second part of the blue's name, sapidus, is the Latin word for flavorful.

The blue crab is the most common crab of the United States Atlantic coast, and, along with the Dungeness, king, and stone crabs, is among the four most commercially important crabs in the United States. Of all crabs marketed in the United States, blues account for about 75 percent.

The meat of the blue crab is tender, sweet, and juicy. The soft-shell stage of the blue crab is believed by some to be the premier seafood of North America. Blue crab meat is available in United States markets alive, freshly cooked, canned, and pasteurized. Blue crab meat may also be purchased frozen, but the meat does not retain its peak of flavor or texture after freezing. A live blue crab is 15 to 25 percent edible meat.

Blue crabs typically displayed in United States markets are 4 to 6 inches across the width of their shells and weigh about 5 ounces. Larger blues are rarely offered. This may be an instance of bigger not being better; some people pass over very large blues as having tougher meat than their smaller cousins.

Blues are caught year round, but the largest catch occurs from late spring to early fall. During the warmer months, blues come inshore from deeper water and are more easily harvested. Almost all soft-shell blues are taken during this time, since blue crabs are relatively inactive during the winter.

The blue crab is extraordinarily prolific and uncommonly adaptable to water and feeding conditions, but blues suffer withering losses from other predators. The female carries between 3/4 and 2 million eggs during spawning, but only a handful of the hatchlings survive. Among the remaining hatchlings, few reach adult size, which occurs in about a year. Adult blue crabs that complete their life cycle have a 2 to 3 year life.

Blues thrive in both salt and fresh waters, as well as brackish shallows. They feed on a variety of plants and animals. In United States waters, the blue crab is most numerous from Cape Cod to the southern tip of Texas. They are especially important commercially in the Chesapeake and Delaware bays with North Carolina and Louisiana not far behind. The Chesapeake Bay area is particularly noted for its harvest of soft-shell blue crabs.

In addition to its strong presence on the United States Atlantic and Gulf coasts, blue crabs have successfully migrated over large distances, often with an unwitting help from man. The blue's primary ticket to adventure has been the ship's ballast, and it can be found in some quantity in most of the world's great harbors. Coincidentally, ship harbors are an ideal entry point for the blue into local waters, since shallow protected waterways are the blue's favored breeding grounds

On the Atlantic side of the Western Hemisphere, blue crabs are occasionally seen as far north as Nova Scotia and as far south as Uruguay. Several colonies of blues thrive in the Bahamas archipelago.

A crab very similar to the blue lives in the Sea of Cortes enclosed by the Baja Peninsula, but its numbers are too small to be important. In Europe, self-perpetuating colonies have established themselves in the Atlantic waters of France, Holland, and Denmark, and in the Mediterranean and Aegean Seas, especially in the areas around the Egyptian, Israeli, and Lebanonese coasts.

The coloration in blue crabs varies, although all are dark. Blue crabs may be dark blue, green, or variegated brown. The undersides are uniformly cream to light tan. Variations in color from male to female are most pronounced on the tips of the claws. Claws on the female are tipped with bright red while the male's pincers are blue and white.

blues: Blue crabs.

brown crab: The brown crab is the most common crab in European Atlantic waters. It is also called the common brown crab. The brown crab is similar to, but smaller and less desirable than the American Dungeness crab.

The meat of the brown crab is tender and flavorful. It is a popular food item frequently encountered along the European Atlantic coast.

buck and rider: A pair of mating crabs.

buckram: A crab in the stage of molting between the paper-shell and the final hardening of the new hard-shell.

buffalo crab: A soft-shell crab that has lost a claw, usually while molting. Some people extend this term to encompass hard-shell crabs with only one claw.

buster: A crab whose shell has split immediately prior to molting. Busters are often set aside in holding tanks to allow the molting process to continue until the crabs become soft-shells.

calico crab: Two species are called calico crabs, one species of which also goes by the name sand crab or lady crab. Occasionally the calico is called the ghost crab. Of the two species, Ovalipes ocellatus ocellatus ranges from Nova Scotia to South Carolina, while the similar Ovalipes ocellatus guadulpensis occupies waters from North Carolina to the Texas Gulf coast.

Both species of calico crabs are small inshore dwellers. They have shells that vary from almost pure white to tan cream; the shells are often marked with red or purple spots.

The meat of the calico is good and flavorful, but the crab is so small, only about 3 inches across, that it is not favored as a food item. Perhaps it would be in greater demand if it did not occupy the same waters as the larger and more plentiful blue crab. The calico is seldom seen at the market.

Calico crabs, when called by the name sand crabs, are sometimes confused with the common sand crab. See common sand crab.

calling crab: See fiddler crab.

carapace: The top shell of the body of a crab. The carapace is often cleaned and used as the container for stuffed or deviled crab dishes.

cases: The body chamber on each side of a crab containing the muscles used to operate the swimming fins. These muscles are the choice lump meat.

chandler: Same as a channeler.

channeler: This term is used interchangeably with whale crab. The word channeler probably entered the language after it was observed that large male crabs were often taken from deeper water, or channels.

chelipeds: The first of the 5 pairs of legs on the crab. On a true crab, this will always be the claws.

cock: A male crab.

coconut crab: See robber crab.

common brown crab: See brown crab.

common crab: In the United States, this refers to the blue crab. In other parts of the world common crab may indicate an altogether different crab, typically the edible crab most plentiful in local waters.

common sand crab (Emerita analoga): The common sand crab is sometimes called the sand crab, a name it shares with the calico crab. With a shared name, confusion is inevitable, but the common sand crab is a very different crab from the calico.

Common sand crabs are very small, seldom growing more than an inch and a quarter across their body. They live in sand on wave-swept beaches and strain their food from water washing over them as the waves run back into the sea.

Although edible when soft-shell, they are seldom taken by man. When eaten, they should be sauteed in the same manner as oyster crabs. Also see porcelain crab.

common shore crab: See green crab.

crab boil: A small sack of spices used to season crabs while boiling. The term also refers to the blended spices themselves. Recipes for crab boil vary, but often include onion, garlic, cloves, salt, and various peppers.

crab pot: This refers to a crab trap, often made of chicken wire and left unattended. Crab pots are often marked by floats constructed of wood or parts of plastic bottles. Floats marking a crab pot may or may not be marked with the owner's name or other identification, but it is a serious breech of conduct if not illegal to tamper with another person's trap.

crib: A floating cage or shallow tank of recirculating salt water where crabs about to molt are kept until they shed their shells and become soft-shells.

cushion: A female crab carrying roe, or eggs.

deadmen: A slang term for the 6 spongy crab's gills located on each side of the crab's body cavity. The word was probably suggested by the gray white color of the organs and by the fact that it they are always removed before eating.

deadmen's fingers: This is used 2 ways, interchangeably with deadmen, and to refer to the crab's legs. After a crab has been boiled or steamed the limp legs of a large crab do bear a superficial resemblance to a skeletal human hand.

decorator crab: The decorator crab is a Pacific crab whose range does not extend to the United States. The decorator is chiefly interesting because of its unique ability to generate a glue that it uses to stick bits and pieces of found materials onto its body. This colorful display serves both to camouflage the crab as well as increase the apparent size of its body, both excellent defense mechanisms.

The decorator has good, edible meat, but is less desirable than other crabs inhabiting the same waters.

deep sea red crab: See red crab.

doubler: A pair of mating crabs.

Dungeness crab (Cancer magister): The Dungeness crab, along with the blue, king, and stone crabs, is among the four most commercially important crabs in the United States.

Dungeness, often mispronounced, is spoken with a soft "g" and the accent on the last syllable. The Dungeness was the first crab fished commercially on the Pacific coast. Its name was taken from the first fishing village on the Pacific coast to engage in the trade. Today the Dungeness is the most popular and commercially important crab on the Pacific coast.

Dungeness crabs were known to the Indians of the Northwest long before the coming of European settlers. Indians trapped these crabs in traps almost identical to the ones used by sport crab fishermen today. Settlers imitated these traps, and soon came to relish Dungeness crabs as a staple in their diets.

The meat of the Dungeness is rich, tender, and distinctively flavored. The color of the meat is white, with the claw meat showing a slight pinkish tint.

The Dungeness is larger than its similarly shaped cousin, the blue crab. Adult crabs have a shell averaging 10 to 12 inches across and a body that is both deep and heavy. Dungeness crabs taken commercially are almost always more than 1 1/2 pounds and crabs of 2 to 3 pounds are not unusual. The ratio of edible meat to the total weight of the Dungeness is 25 to 33 percent, a high ratio. Dungeness caught inshore are usually smaller than those taken from the open sea.

The Dungeness ranges the Pacific coast from the Aleutian Islands to Baja, California. The species is most numerous from the southern tip of Alaska to the southern California coast. The area around Monterey Bay, California, is especially rich.

Dungeness crabs prefer areas with gentle tides and sandy, grass-covered bottoms. Inshore catches are typically at 10-foot depths; offshore catches range from 125 to 250 feet deep.

The Dungeness is a relatively long-lived member of the rock crab family, reaching maturity after 4 years and living as long as 8. By comparison with another commercially important crab, the blue crab seldom lives longer than 2 to 3 years.

The shell of the Dungeness is brown tending to reddish or purplish hues. The underside is whitish, often tending to light orange or yellow. The crab's rear legs may be streaked with crimson or purple.

Since this is the most common crab on the Pacific coast, it is sometimes called the market crab there.

elbow crab (Heterocrypta occidentalis): The elbow crab is a very small crab. Its maximum growth is less than an inch and a half. It is almost never eaten by man. Inhabiting mainly tropical waters, it is seen on United States shores only in southernmost California.

fat crab: A crab as it approaches the molting period and prepares to shed its outer shell. Also describes the crab between the buckram and peeler phases.

fiddler crab (Uca crenulata): This distant, diminutive relative of the stone crab seldom grows larger than 1 inch. It is seldom eaten by man and is of no commercial importance.

The fiddler takes its name from the characteristic sizes of the claws of the male crab, one claw very large and the other tiny. The large claw probably suggests a fiddle while the smaller one suggests the fiddle's bow. Actually, the claws serve no musical function nor are they even noisemakers. The large claw's primary purpose appears to be to assist the male during mating battles and as an aid in establishing territories. While mating, the male fiddler may shed its typical mottled brown color to display iridescent purples and blues.

Fiddlers live in mud and sand burrows in warm, tropical waters. The crabs adapt well to a variety of water conditions, but are especially numerous in Florida along the United States coast of the Gulf of Mexico, and in the hook of Cape Cod. They are largely nocturnal but are often observed during daylight hours scooting rapidly along shallow bottoms.

The fiddler crab is also known as the calling crab, marsh fiddler, and red-jointed fiddler crab. The species comprises an important source of food for coastal birds.

flake crab meat: Small pieces of white crab meat. These are smaller than lump meat, which comes from the large swimming muscles. Typically, flake crab meat is less expensive than lump meat.

flat porcelain crab: See porcelain crab.

ghost crab: See calico crab.

globose kelp crab: See kelp crab.

golden crab: See red crab.

granceola: A Mediterranean expression for soft-shell crabs. While soft-shell crabs in the United States are almost always blue crabs, this is not necessarily true in Mediterranean countries.

green crab: A term that may have any of three meanings: (1) a species of crab (Carcinides maenas), (2) any crab bought alive, or (3) a crab due to shed its hard, outer shell in a week to 10 days.

The green crab is also known as the common shore crab, green shore crab, and shore crab. It is a swimming crab with a dark green shell, often punctuated by splashes of yellow. The green crab obtains an adult growth of about 3 inches.

The green crab also lives in British and French waters from which it migrated to the United States, probably by way of trading ships, shortly after colonial times. The crab is now firmly established on the Atlantic seaboard from Maine to New Jersey.

Green crabs are more a curse than a blessing to the fishing industry. Green crabs are burrowing as well as swimming crabs, and have a marked taste for soft clams which they consume in large numbers. The United States soft clam industry is significantly harmed by their presence.

Green crabs are not important commercially, although their meat is delicately flavored and finely textured. If the green crab were larger or if it did not inhabit the same waters as the more important blue crab, perhaps it would be in greater demand. In Europe, the green crab is a popular and aggressively marketed food item.

A similar species, Carcinides mediterraneus, is native to the Mediterranean. Two very small crabs, the striped shore crab and the purple shore crab, inhabit United States Pacific coastal waters, but neither of these crabs grows beyond 2 inches and neither is important commercially.

green shore crab: See green crab.

Gulf crab: See red crab.

hair crab: The hair crab is similar to, but smaller than the king crab. Like the king crab, the hair crab is a deep-water walking crab with long legs growing on a relatively small body.

The hair crab inhabits the same Bering Sea ranges as the king, but unlike king crabs, adult hair crabs only attain growth of between 2 and 3 pounds. The hair crab is very popular in Japan where it commands high prices at market. The United States market for hair crabs is inactive.

The hair crab is also known as the kegani crab, Korean crab, and Pacific hair crab.

hair-sign crab: A crab in the very early stage of molting, when the first signs of the color changes caused by the molting process occur.

hairy hermit crab: See hermit crab.

hard-shell crab: Any crab with a hard shell, but the term usually describes the blue crab during the part of its life cycle when the shell is hard. See soft-shell crab.

hen: A female crab.

hermit crab: The hermit crab is a crustacean, but is not a true crab. It is distantly related to the robber crab.

Hermit crabs are distinctive in that they grow no shells of their own but borrow snail shells, moving into successively larger ones as they grow. Occasionally hermits will be seen moving around in something more colorful than another creature's discarded house. The hermit will set up housekeeping in almost anything that is hollow and about the right size, including small bottles and other castoffs.

Most hermits are aquatic, but a few species in this group are terrestrials. It strikes me as a bizarre practice, but I have heard of people attaching a hermit's adopted shell to their clothing and wearing the living crab as a piece of ornamental jewelry.

Hermit crabs are not an important food source for man, but can be eaten after frying or roasting. I do not recommend eating hermit crabs raw. Hermits found inshore are invariably small, but in the deep waters of the Pacific one species, the hairy hermit crab, may grow up to 4 inches.

horseshoe crab (Limulus polyphemus): The horseshoe is not a true crab at all, in fact it is not even a crustacean. The horseshoe crab is very much like what it looks like, a 200-million-year-old survivor of the Paleozoic era. It is more closely related to those creatures, now long dead, that first crawled out of the sea onto the land. Scientifically, it is classed with the arachnids.

As if this evolutionary novelty were not unusual enough, the horseshoe crab has two pairs of eyes, one simple and the other compound. The horseshoe takes its name from the shape of its body, roughly the shape of a horse's foot. Sir Walter Raleigh reported from the New World that the Indians called the creature "see-ekanauk," and used its long, rigid tail as a tip for their fishing spears.

There are 5 species of horseshoe crabs living on the Atlantic coast of North America and in East Asian waters. All the species appear much the same, having heavily armored brown shells with long spiked tails. They are very poor swimmers and usually crawl on the bottom foraging for small bits of food.

Horseshoe crabs grow up to 22 inches long. They are harmless to man, though startling when stepped on by a careless wader.

The horseshoe crab is sometimes called the king crab, but it should not to be confused with the edible, large king crabs of the northern Pacific.

Horseshoe crabs are not eaten by man.

hotel: A size category used when referring to soft-shell blue crabs. A hotel size crab measures from 4 to 4 1/2 inches across the widest part of its body.

Japanese crab: See king crab.

jimmy crab: A male crab, also called a jimmy dick or a jimmy channeler.

Jonah crab (Cancer borealis): The Jonah crab is a walking crab favoring the open areas of the Continental Shelf off the New England coast. During the spring months these crabs come inshore among the rocks and shallows from Maine to Long Island. Jonahs are a popular catch for amateur fishermen, and can be recognized by a dark red to purple red top shell. The bottom of the shell is cream tending toward yellow.

The Jonah is similar to, but slightly larger than rock crabs inhabiting the same waters. The Jonah crab typically measures from 4 to 6 inches wide, with the larger crabs weighing just over a pound.

Jonahs have excellent meat but for a variety of reasons are seldom encountered in markets. Inshore Jonahs inhabit the same waters as the more popular blue crabs and the more profitable lobster. Being a walking crab, the Jonah does not offer a crabber the pocket of valuable and easily extracted lump meat muscle that operates the swimming fins of the blue crab. As a result, almost a dozen Jonah crabs must be hand picked to obtain a pound of crab meat. In addition, the meat obtained comes out in smaller pieces that are less valued by the market.

Most of the meat of Jonahs is picked by the families of lobstermen and is sold close to the source. Jonah crabs are an accidental catch brought in by the lobstermen as they go about their work. In the past, many Jonahs have simply been returned to the sea. One interesting story concerning these lobstermen is that they gave the Jonah its name after comparing the way it walked into their traps with the biblical story of Jonah being swallowed by the whale.

Fishing boats harvesting the Jonah populations over the Continental Shelf must be specially equipped with on-board processing plants, without which too much of the catch dies before it can be landed. As more boatmen make this capital investment, Jonahs should become more familiar to consumers. Considering the size of the population of Jonahs living in close proximity to East Coast fishing centers, the meat of this crab should become increasingly important.

Jonah meat offered in the market is typically less expensive than blue crab meat. The best available usually comes from the claws. In limited quantities, Jonah crab meat is available fresh, frozen, or pasteurized.

In addition to the New England coastal area, Jonahs range from Nova Scotia to Florida. A similar crab inhabits the Bahamas archipelago but displays a yellow-tinged shell with red spots. The largest concentration of Jonahs is the United States Continental Shelf at depths up to 2,500 feet. The scientific name of the Jonah crab is Latin for northern crab.

jumbo: A size category of used when referring to soft-shell blue crabs. A jumbo size crab measures from 5 to 5 1/2 inches across the widest part of its body.

keeper: A crab at or over the legal size above which it may be kept. Crabs below this limit must be returned to the water. The size of a keeper varies from state to state and species to species.

kegani crab: See hair crab.

kelp crab: Two species of kelp crabs are seen in United States waters, both on the Pacific coast. The first, the shield backed kelp crab (Pugettia producta), grows to about 4 inches. Its shell coloring is dark green, often with red spots.

The second kelp crab, globose kelp crab (Taliepus nuttalli), is slightly larger than the shield back and grows a red colored shell. The globose lives in relatively deep water. Neither kelp crab is importantly commercially, although both are edible.

king crab (Paralithodes camtschatica): King crab is sometimes used to refer to the horseshoe crab (inedible), but the more common use is in reference to large walking crabs native to the frigid northern waters of the Pacific Ocean, and the Bering and Okhotsk seas. The king crab is, along with the blue, Dungeness, and stone crabs, among the four most commercially important crabs in the United States. The king crab is also known as the Alaska king crab, Japanese crab, and Russian crab. A similar crab of no commercial importance to the United States, Paralithodes antarctica, inhabits cold southern waters.

This species takes its scientific name from the Greek para, meaning closely resembling, then adds lithodes, Greek for stone, and referring to the stone-like appearance of its body shell.

The term, camtschatica, was suggested by the Kamchatka Peninsula of the Soviet Union, long a fertile hunting ground for this variety of crab.

King crabs are deep water crabs. They are also walking crabs; they cannot even swim. Compared to inshore crabs like the blue, Dungeness, or stone crabs, kings have very undeveloped claws.

The season for harvesting king crabs is during the worst period of Arctic midwinter, when the king's molting season begins and the crabs move from their summer feeding grounds in the icy, 1,000-

foot depths, to relatively shallow 50- to 300-foot range. It is hearty work, calling for strong, well-trained crews.

The crabs are caught by a fleet equipped with gigantic pots or traps the size of a walk-in closet and half as high. The traps are lowered from the sides of the ship and rest on the bottom. They are equipped with escape holes for young or small crabs. Only large males are kept; in the interest of conservation, the rest are released. Although 20-pound monsters have been taken, the average size king crab is just over 10 pounds and about 5 feet from leg tip to leg tip.

Even though the king crab fishing season occurs when the unprotected Arctic seas are roughest and most dangerous, the most modern ships are equipped to process the crab catch on board within minutes of capture. Before a crab caught by a processing ship sees land, it will have been cleaned, cooked, frozen, and packaged.

King crabs captured by a fishing ship that does not have on-board processing facilities are kept in circulating holding tanks. Brought to shore alive, they are then processed by land-based plants on the Alaskan coast.

The king's useful meat is found in the claws, shoulders, and especially, the legs. About 25 percent of the total weight of the crab is edible. Fresh king crab meat is almost never available far from the Alaskan coast. King crab is sold canned or as crab legs precooked and frozen in the shell. The latter is unusually tasty.

King crab meat is white with pinkish edges. It is flavorful, but relatively coarse compared to the meat of the Dungeness or blue crabs. King crab meat is more suited for use in cooked dishes than in salads or other recipes calling for a finely textured meat.

Kona crab: The Kona is a popular and delicately flavored crab from Hawaiian waters. It is seldom seen in mainland markets.

Korean crab: See hair crab.

lady crab: See calico crab.

land crab (Cardisoma guanhumi): The land crab is an excellent illustration of the way names become confusing when talking about crabs. The land crab is also known as the white crab, the mulatto crab, and, in the Caribbean, as the black crab. Of all these names, I think that land crab is most appropriate because this little critter does in fact live on the land, returning to the sea only periodically.

Land crabs are native to the United States along the Gulf coast from Florida to Texas. They live throughout the Caribbean, and their land-to-sea migrations have become the subject of festivals and holidays in Cuba, the Bahamas, and Jamaica. They are about the same size as the blue crab and just as flavorful. Cooking is identical to water crabs.

I have seen only one land crab. While visiting friends in the Caribbean, the family dog put up a ruckus that drew us into the backyard. The dog was worrying an especially large and ugly looking crab in the middle of the yard. The dog in this case was actually a big clumsy puppy, and there was never any doubt about the outcome of the contest. Much barking, jumping, and one nipped nose later the crab scampered away leaving the dog a sadder and more cautious fellow. Still, I understand why land crabs are seldom seen today in populated areas. A crab on land is not much of a match for a human or even a well-educated, large dog. In most areas, land crabs are almost extinct.

lid: The top shell of the body of a crab; also called the carapace. The lid is often cleaned and used as the container for stuffed or deviled crab dishes.

lemon crab: A female crab carrying roe, or eggs.

lump crab meat: The largest and most desirable pieces of meat from the body of the crab. Lump meat is found on each side of the body of the crab. It is the muscle that operates the swimming fins.

maneaters: The gills of the crab. The gills are always removed before eating.

market crab: See Dungeness crab.

marsh fiddler: See fiddler crab.

masking crab (Loxorhynchus crispatus): A species of crab that hangs a disguise of algae, seaweed, and sponge from a series of thorny spines growing from its shell. Masking crabs seldom grow more than 3 inches across their shells. Distantly related crabs that grow to much larger sizes practice the same sort of camouflage when small, but as they grow larger they discontinue the practice.

Masking crabs inhabit Pacific waters. They are colorful, but not important commercially.

medium: A size category of used when referring to soft-shell blue crabs. A medium-size crab measures from 3 1/2 to 4 inches across the widest part of its body.

Morro crab: See stone crab.

mud crab: See stone crab.

mulatto crab: See land crab.

mussel crab: See oyster crab.

nicking a crab: Breaking the movable fingers of the claws to prevent their use. Nicking a crab renders the crab helpless. It is often done to make crabs easier to handle or to prevent the crabs from fighting and killing one another while in holding containers.

number 1s: The largest size blue crabs; also called whale crabs.

ocean bay crab: Used to refer to the larger specimens of Dungeness crabs. This term entered the language because the Dungeness crabs taken from the open sea were larger than crabs caught in bays and estuaries.

orange crab: A female crab carrying roe, or eggs.

oyster crab (Pinnotheres subquadrata): The oyster crab, though tiny, possesses a flavor unmatched in sweetness and delicacy. The name is derived from the fact that the female crab lives inside the shell of oysters, maintaining a soft shell that does not harm the host. The male of the species lives in open water and does develop a hard shell except when molting.

The oyster crab, and closely related cousins, live on both the Atlantic and Pacific coasts. Collectively, they may also be called the pea crab, mussel crab, or American mussel crab.

Even the largest oyster crabs are tiny, about the size of an average fingernail, with smooth, polished shells. Typically they are almost transparent and range in color from a delicate rose pink to a ghost-like gray white.

The most highly prized oyster crabs come from the Pacific Northwest. They are often sold, when you can find them, processed in cans or bottles. Occasionally in very large cities with active specialty markets, oyster crabs will be available fresh, by weight. The supply is very limited.

Oyster crabs are eaten whole, including the shell. They are highly prized by gourmets as an ingredient in oyster stews, as a garnish, and for use in certain fish sauces. Oyster crabs may be eaten sauteed or fried. Although I do not recommend it, oyster crabs are sometimes eaten raw.

Pacific hair crab: See hair crab.

palm crab: See robber crab.

paper-shell crab: A molting crab between the soft-shell and buckram stage of shell hardening. A paper-shell crab has normally completed molting 9 to 12 hours prior.

pea crab: See oyster crab.

peeler: A crab in the early stage of molting. The hard shell has not yet cracked open, but the underlying soft-shell is fully formed.

pine crab: A tiny tree-dwelling crab. It lives in water that collects in hollows of plants in tropical rain forests. It has no commercial or food value to man.

pink-rim crab: The stage of molting following the white-rim. In this condition the crab exhibits a thin pink line on the inner border of the back fin. A pink-rim crab will probably molt within a week.

porcelain crab: Porcelain crabs are members of the common sand crab group of crabs. All are small; the largest of the porcelain crabs grows only to about 1 inch across the shell. The three principal groups of porcelain crabs are the porcelain sand crab (Lepidopa myops), the flat porcelain crab (Petrolisthes cinctipes), and the thick clawed porcelain crab (Pachycheles rudis). Their name is derived from the porcelain crab's blue white, china-like color, although some less common varieties are brownish red.

Porcelain crabs are edible, especially in the soft-shell stage, although they are seldom taken by man. If cooked, they should be sauteed and prepared in the same manner as oyster crabs.

porcelain sand crab: See porcelain crab.

prime: A size category of used when referring to soft-shell blue crabs. A prime size crab measures from 4 1/2 to 5 inches across the widest part of its body.

punk: A female crab carrying roe, or eggs.

purple shore crab: See green crab.

queen crab: See spider crab.

Queensland mud crab: As the name suggests, the Queensland mud crab is an Australian crab. Many gourmets in the southern Pacific area believe that it is the most delicately flavored crab in the region. The Queensland mud crab is not marketed in the United States.

rank peeler: The stage of molting just before the shell begins to crack.

red crab (Geryon quinquedens): This is gruesome enough. The red crab's Latin name means a three-bodied monster (Geryon) with five teeth (quinquedens). Doesn't sound like something that you'd want to meet on a dark night dive, does it?

Fanciful crab namers aside, the red crab is practically always encountered on a plate rather than in a nightmare. Almost all the red crab meat available to retail consumers has been precooked, and you are unlikely to see one in the inshore shallows. Red crabs live in both Atlantic and Pacific waters, but they are most common along the Eastern seaboard in the cold, icy depths below 1,500 feet. Further south in warmer waters, the red crab maintains its preference for the cold and descends to over 7,000 feet. The red crab is caught at these depths by fishermen using deep water pots and traps.

They are occasionally trawled. Red crab meat is new to the market, though the meat is desirable. Red crab meat is perishable, and only recently have the fishing fleets been willing to invest in the shipboard refrigeration tanks and processing facilities needed to maintain the quality of the catch on the way to market.

Red crabs have a top weight of about 3 pounds for males and roughly 1 pound for females. Both crabs are about 25 percent meat. The meat is white with a slight pink tint reminiscent of the king crab. Red crab meat is still picked mostly by hand and is rarely available except frozen.

The red crab is, as its name suggests, a red orange to dark red color. The underside is cream to tan. The red crab may also be called the deep sea red crab. The red crab has a tan-colored cousin found in Gulf waters, sometimes referred to as the golden crab or the Gulf crab.

A separate species of crab, Pleuroncodes planipes, is also known as the red crab. It is sometimes called the squat lobster or tuna crab. The home of this crab is the open sea off the Southern California coast. They come inshore only when caught by a freak of wind or current. They grow to a maximum size of only 5 inches and are not important commercially.

red-jointed fiddler: See fiddler crab.

red rock crab: See rock crab.

red-sign peeler: The stage of molting following the pink-rim. In this condition the crab exhibits a thin red line on the inner border of the back fin. A red-sign peeler will probably molt within 2 days.

red zodiac crab: An eastern Atlantic crab. The red zodiac crab is flavorful and enjoys great popularity in England and western Europe.

retread: When a stone crab has a claw removed and is returned to the water, it will grow a replacement claw. Regenerated claws are normally smaller than the first growth. A retread is a stone crab that has grown or is in the process of growing a replacement claw.

robber crab (Birgus latro): The robber crab is one of the most interesting crabs in the world. It is native to the Pacific and Indian oceans area. It is not a true crab, being distantly related to the hermit crab. It is protected by bony backplates rather than the crab's familiar shell. The robber crab is also known as the birgus crab, coconut crab, palm crab, and tree crab, and with good reason. This adventuresome creature not only has a taste for young coconuts, but likes to climb the coconut tree and pick its dinner fresh.

Robber crabs grow to more than a foot long and climb the coconut trees by grasping the trunk with their feet and inching their way up. Once up the tree, the crab uses its powerful claws to cut the coconut loose. On the ground, the coconut is opened and eaten. The young find food by scavenging after the older, larger crabs.

Robber crabs are a popular source of food to many Pacific island natives. They may also be a source of amusement. These awkward little fellows were hardly designed by nature to be tree climbers. Without doubt gravity and clumsiness takes a fearsome toll both on the way up and back down. Now, picture a group of Pacific islanders watching a bunch of cruise passengers picnicing under a beach palm...

rock crab: The rock crab belongs to the same family as the Dungeness, Jonah, and many of the most popular European crab varieties. It is found in both Atlantic (Cancer irroratus) and Pacific (Cancer productus) inshore waters. Sometimes it is called the big crab. The rock crab's upper shell is light red, often with purple or reddish spots. On the West Coast, there is a more deeply colored rock crab that is sometimes called the red rock crab.

Although rock crab meat is flavorful and finely textured, it is not commonly marketed. In addition, the rock crab native to Atlantic waters is only about 4 inch wide, so small that many people believe the rock crab is more trouble to clean and pick than the meat is worth; the rock crab of the Pacific may grow to 7 inches, but it is still not highly prized commercially. A similar Pacific crab, the spot-bellied rock crab is even smaller.

When sold live, rock crabs are usually considerably less expensive than blue or Dungeness crabs that occupy the same waters.

Rock crab meat makes an excellent and tasty addition to soups, stews, gumbos, or for use in combination with other fish products.

roe: Crab eggs, typically colored red, orange, or red orange. The female carries the eggs beneath the apron, or tail, located on the back underside of the crab. The number of eggs carried by a female crab varies by species. The blue crab carries 750,000 to 2,000,000 eggs per spawning Only a handful of the hatchlings survive longer than a few days. Although it is illegal in almost all jurisdictions to take egg-bearing females, roe is considered a delicacy, and is an essential ingredient in the famed she-crab soup of South Carolina.

Russian crab: See king crab.

sally: An immature female crab. Sometimes sally is used interchangeably with sook. Sallys can be identified by the tab underneath the crab; the tab of an immature female crab will be triangular.

Samoan crab: The Samoan is native to Hawaiian waters. It is commonly marketed in Hawaii but seldom available in mainland markets.

sand crab: See calico crab, also see common sand crab.

second: A crab in the process of molting, 3 to 5 days before shedding its outer shell.

she-crab: A female crab, especially a female crab bearing eggs.

shield backed kelp crab: See kelp crab.

shore crab: See green crab.

snot crab: A crab in the process of molting, 7 to 10 days before shedding its outer shell.

snow crab: See spider crab.

soft-shell crab: Any crab that has shed its hard, outer shell in preparation for a new one, but most often used when referring to blue crabs. Soft-shell crabs comprise about 2.5 percent of the total blue crab catch. Soft-shell begin to harden about 2 hours after exposure to salt water. After about 2 days, hardening is complete.

While in a soft-shell condition, crabs are extremely vulnerable to predators, including man. Some gourmets believe that a properly prepared soft-shell crab is the premier American seafood. Generally speaking, the softer the shell, the more desirable the crab is for the table.

sook: An adult female crab. Sometimes sook is used interchangeably with sally.

spider crab: Spider crab is the name for the Chionoecetes genus of crabs. There are four principal varieties available in the United States, the snow crab (Chionoecetes opilio) and its slightly larger cousin (Chionoecetes bairdi), the tanner crab (Chionoecetes tanneti), and (Chionoecetes angulatus), a very deep water crab typically encountered at 6,000 feet and beyond. Crabs of this genus are also sometimes referred to as queen crabs. The thornback, familiar in Europe, also a spider crab, is especially prized in France and Spain.

Actually, the names snow crab, tanner crab, and queen crab are marketing inventions. The name spider was found to have a negative influence on sales. The spider crab may also be sold under the names Alaska snow crab and Atlantic snow crab.

The snow and tanner crabs are very similar to king crabs, but on a slightly smaller scale, averaging between 1 and 5 pounds and usually less than 3 feet from leg tip to leg tip. They have a preference for cold waters but usually feed in more shallow areas than the king. Also like the king crabs, spiders are walking crabs with long, slender legs and tiny finger-like claws. They swim poorly or not at all. They have small bodies and almost all of the usable meat comes from the legs.

Most spider crabs caught for the United States market are fished by the same fleets that also harvest the larger king crab. They are fished primarily in the northern Pacific from the Bering Sea to Washington, although some tanners are taken as far south as Mexico. Catches are made similarly to king crab catches, by deep sea pots and traps dropped by ships equipped with floating processing plants or holding tanks to return the catch alive to land-based processing plants in Alaska.

The color, texture, and taste of spider crab meat is almost identical to king crab and is a ready substitute when king crab catches are low.

sponge: A female crab carrying roe, or eggs.

sponge crab: A species of crab common in southern Pacific waters. The sponge crab uses its claws to cut out a sponge sheet that it holds over its body as camouflage. The sponge crab does not inhabit United States waters.

spot-bellied rock crab: See rock crab.

squat lobster: See red crab.

stone crab (Menippi mercenaria): The stone crab, along with the blue, Dungeness, and king crabs, is among the four most commercially important crabs in the United States. Its meat is located principally in the claws. The meat of the stone crab is rich, sweet, and firm, and it is thought by some to be the best crab meat available anywhere in the world.

Stone crabs are found from the coast of North Carolina south to the Gulf of Mexico and west to the coast of Texas. The center of stone crab trade is in Florida where by all accounts the best, most delicately flavored stone crabs are harvested.

Among crabs, the stone crab is relatively long-lived; ages of 8 to 10 years are not uncommon. The shell of the adult stone crab is about 5 inches across and 2 inches deep, thick for a crab. Typically, the shells are purplish to dark brown, with some displaying reddish hues. The crab's legs have red and yellow bands and are more suitable for walking than swimming.

The stone crab's meaty claws are a delicate cream and coral tipped with a splash of black. In the adult, they are about 3 to 4 inches long

The stone crab took its name from both the hardness and from the stone-like appearance of its body shell. Anyone who has tried to crack open the body of a stone crab (illegal, by the way) will surely agree that it is just about like cracking a stone. If for some reason you need to do it, a hammer is the best tool.

Most stone crabs caught for commercial sale are taken with traps, but the meat is so good that almost every weekend crab fisherman along the Gulf coast gets into the act. Be careful if you handle these little critters. They are not at all glad to see you and exhibit a cross temper when removed from the water. Their claws are powerful and can inflict a very painful wound. It may be my imagination, but they look like they want to hurt someone.

Be sure to check local fishing laws before crabbing for stone crabs. In many, if not all places, it is illegal to keep the whole crab. When a stone crab is caught, the fisherman should break off the dominant, or larger claw, and return the crab to the sea where it will grow a new one. A lost claw does not inhibit the crab; the claws of the stone crab are purely defensive.

Breaking a claw from a stone crab is much less cruel than it sounds. In fact, the stone crab, in common with its cousins, has the ability to cast off its own injured or caught legs, including the claws.

Through reflex action, a crab can and often does shed one of its own legs at any of several naturally occurring joints. The old leg is dropped off and a new, regenerated leg or claw is grown to replace the lost member. The process is called autotomy, and can be repeated 3 or 4 times for each appendage. Regeneration takes about 18 months.

Autotomy is not at all the painful or messy business of the proverbial wolf chewing off its own paw rather than being caught in a trap. Autotomy actually is a benefit to the crab. Relative to the crab's body, its long, exposed legs are especially vulnerable to damage or attack. The ability of the crab to discard and renew its legs is one of the reasons the crab has been with us so long and thrives in so many diverse parts of the sea.

The stone crab is also known as the mud crab, and on some of the Caribbean islands as the Morro crab. It is a member of the mud crab family.

striped shore crab: See green crab.

Surimi: Common market term for imitation crabmeat.

sweet-water crab: A crab living in fresh water. Many species of crabs are quite versatile and capable of living in fresh, salt, or brackish water. A few species live almost exclusively in fresh water.

swimming crab: This term may refer to any of a large number of crabs equipped with swimming fins on the last pair of legs. They are distinct from the walking crabs, many of which swim poorly if at all. Many swimming crabs have well-developed muscles supporting the swimming fins. These muscles constitute the most expensive grade of crab meat, the highly prized lump meat. The most commercially important swimming crab is the blue crab.

Swimming crab is also used to refer to a species of crab, Portunus xantusii. These small blue gray crabs are too small to be commercially important; their mature growth is only 2 to 3 inches. Swimming crabs live in Pacific coastal waters, and unlike most species of crabs, have razor sharp claws. In spite of their small size, crabs must be handled carefully or they can inflict painful cuts.

"T": The large triangular section section on the underside of the crab; also the apron. In the female, this is used to protect the eggs.

tab: The same as the "T", or the apron.

tablier: The same as the "T", or the apron.

tanner crab: See spider crab.

Tasmanian crab: The Tasmanian crab is one of the deep water southern Pacific crabs. It is not marketed in the United States. The meat is edible but more coarsely textured and far less desirable than that of the Queensland mud crab available in the same region. The Tasmanian crab's claim to distinction is its size, up to 30 pounds.

thick-clawed porcelain crab: See porcelain crab.

thornback crab: See spider crab.

tinback: A molting crab with a soft shell that has almost completed the hardening process. The name is probably derived from the sensation of feeling thin metal while holding the crab.

tomalley: The liver of the crab. The tomalley is less familiar than white or brown crab meat, but it is edible and tasty. Tomalley varies widely in color; it may be green, brown, or even orange when raw; when cooked, tomalley changes color to dark red. Highly prized by some cooks.

tree crab: See robber crab.

tuna crab: See red crab.

water gall crab: A molting crab in the stage between the soft-shell and buckram, 9 to 12 hours after molting. Sometimes called a white crab or windjammer crab.

whale: Whales are the largest size soft-shell blue crabs, measuring more than 5 1/2 inches at their widest point. Whales are also called Number 1s, channelers, and other names. Some people use whale crab to refer to male crabs only, probably since the male crab is larger than the female in almost all species.

white crab: See land crab. White crab may also refer to the stage of molting between the soft-shell and buckram, 9 to 12 hours after molting.

white-rim crab: A crab due to molt and shed its hard outer shell in 7 to 10 days.

windjammer crab: A molting crab in the stage between the soft-shell and buckram, 9 to 12 hours after molting. Sometimes called a water gall crab or a white crab.

A

B

C

Glenn Day is an avid cook and traveler. His fondness for other seafood was previously seen in *Simply Shrimp*, published by The Crossing Press in 1990. He currently resides in Arlington, Texas.

THE CROSSING PRESS
publishes a full line of cookbooks.
For a free catalog, call toll-free

800 / 777-1048

Please specify a *cookbook* catalog.